BRITISH ARTEFACTS

Volume 3
Late Saxon, Late Viking & Norman

(AD 950-1150)

By the same author

British Artefacts Volume 1 – Early Anglo-Saxon
British Artefacts Volume 2 – Middle Saxon & Viking
Wayland's Work – Anglo-Saxon Art and Material Culture from the 4th to the 7th Century
(in collaboration with Stephen Pollington and Lindsay Kerr)

Dedication

For Robert Hallett, one could not wish for a better friend

Acknowledgements

In researching this third volume in the series I have called upon the advice and expertise of many friends and colleagues, too numerous to specify individually. I must, however, mention Alan and Dan Golbourn, Stephen Pollington and Laird Landmann. Thanks
are due to Damir Radic, who assisted with aspects of the design and layout of the book.

Picture credits:
TimeLine Auctions, UK
TimeLine Originals, UK
Musée de la Tapisserie de Bayeux
Metropolitan Museum of Art, New York
Lindsay Kerr - line drawings p.107, fig.2.6.1-a
Roy Turland - Chapes Research Project line drawings

Front cover: hilt of a 10th century Viking sword
Back cover: 10th century Viking trefoil brooch
Inside Back Cover: Norman Helmet

Contents

Maps

Note: The maps have been provided as a general guide to artefact distributions, based on the finds reported to the PAS and on detector finds published in the press and on relevant websites. It is likely that some areas are under-reported either due to low metal-detecting activity or the absence of a local PAS contact. The maps should therefore be taken as an indication of finds distributions based on an unquantifiable level of reporting activity.

Published by Greenlight Publishing,
The Publishing House, 119 Newland Street,
Witham, Essex CM8 1WF

Tel: 01376 521900
Fax: 01376 521901

mail@greenlightpublishing.co.uk
www.greenlightpublishing.co.uk

Editor Greg Payne

Origination Damir Radić

ISBN 978 1 897738 504

Printed in Great Britain

© 2013 Brett Hammond, TimeLine Originals

BRITISH ARTEFACTS
Volume 3 - Late Saxon, Late Viking & Norman

The Late Saxon, Late Viking and Norman period is crucially important in the story of England. The ruling families of all but one Anglo-Saxon kingdom were swept away by the Scandinavian adventurers: only Wessex survived the attacks of these Viking war bands and the West Saxon kings consolidated their power and began the process of re-conquest of the Danelaw. Danish interest in the kingdom did not decline, and by the early 11th century, England came under the rule of its first Danish king Cnut (Canute).

During Cnut's reign, England was drawn into the internal wars of the Danes and Norwegians. After his death, powerful families took the reins of power in England, Denmark, Norway and the newly-founded state of Normandy. The interactions and rivalry between these kindreds led to the accession of King Harold Godwinesson, the last Viking invasion of 1066, the Norman invasion of 1066 and the transformation of English society under Norman rulers.

In this significant book, Brett Hammond builds on the success of the previous volumes, illustrating the social, military, economic and religious developments in the Late Saxon, Late Viking and Norman periods with well-chosen artefacts of many types photographed to bring out their beauty and charm.

The author is a respected researcher in the field of Anglo-Saxon and Viking material culture, with more than a decade at the forefront of object identification and classification. His fascination with and passion for the subject comes through on every page.

British Artefacts is a new series of books covering finds made in the British Isles and their contexts, drawing on parallel Continental examples. The objects described and illustrated (in photographs and line-drawings) will represent the range of items in use, from the lowly pin or knife blade to the finest quality jewellery.

Foreword

by Dr. Ronald Bonewitz

Dr Ronald Bonewitz has had a lifelong interest in archaeology and the ancient world. Originally trained as a geologist, he was a consultant on archaeological investigations in the south-western USA. Also interested in Mesoamerica and befriended by living Maya, he was frequently taken to then-unrecorded Mayan ruins. Since moving to the UK, for the past 30 years he has engaged in archaeological surveying and field walking, and has been connected to the Butser Iron Age Farm Reconstruction, and the Weald and Downland Museum project. He is the author of four books for the Smithsonian Institution; amongst his many other titles are a book on Egyptian Hieroglyphics, a book on the Maya 'prophecy', and others on the ancient Egyptians and the Maya.

I was very pleased to be asked to write a foreword to this latest book in the *British Artefacts* series. Since moving to the UK in the 1970s, I have been privileged to be able to follow my archaeological interests in entirely new directions with a particular interest in Roman, Medieval, Saxon and Viking periods.

I first encountered Brett Hammond when it became necessary to sell part of my extensive collection to finance an internet venture. On meeting him I found him to not only be personable, but highly knowledgeable and a person of high professional standards. Subsequent dealings with TimeLine have only reinforced those impressions. Later, as a consultant with TimeLine on gems, minerals, and fossils, I have now had a chance to meet many of the highly motivated professionals that are part of the TimeLine team. Seeing this book in progress has yet again reinforced my admiration for the high standards and expertise that surrounds Brett. I am equally impressed with the large professional library that supports the research that has gone into every item in these volumes.

The author's other contributions to the literature include *British Artefacts*: Volumes 1 and 2; co-authorship of *Wayland's Work*; more than 70 magazine features and articles; and a soon-to-be published book on posy rings. To write with authority and erudition on such a diverse range demands a broad sweep of knowledge and familiarity with his subjects. He has acquired those attributes thanks to more than three decades of senior management. At TimeLine Originals and TimeLine Auctions he has initiated a project to build an archive of high resolution images and accompanying identification data sourced from the many thousands of coins and artefacts that have passed through the company's catalogues, and ably supported in this series by well-researched text. This positions him at the forefront among experts in those fields. Greenlight's ability to coordinate, edit and publish the material in very reasonably priced volumes helps to enhance the availability of these informative and highly usable books for archaeologists, researchers, conservators, collectors, FLOs, and detectorists.

Anyone who reads it will surely join me in expressing their enthusiasm for *British Artefacts: Volume 3*; and for the monumental amounts of work Brett Hammond as author and Greenlight as publisher have put into of what is evolving into an encyclopedic survey of the material culture of the British Isles.

Introduction to the Series

British Artefacts is an ongoing series of books covering English and British finds and their contexts. Each title will cover a specific period or date-range. The objects described and illustrated (by photographs or by museum-quality artwork) represent the range of items in use, from the lowly pin or knife-blade to the finest quality jewellery.

The books show the developing 'material culture' of England viewed through the artefacts which remain to us. Material culture is an academic term meaning the physical output of blacksmiths, glassmakers, potters, stonemasons, scribes, boneworkers, illuminators, goldsmiths, leatherworkers, woodworkers and all the thousands upon thousands of individuals who supported these specialist craftworkers in their various endeavours. Without the tanner, the leatherworker would have no materials; without the herdsman and the slaughterman, the tanner would also be idle. All these craftsmen were fed by the work of ploughmen and hunters, shepherds and fishermen, millers and bakers. For every item we now have to admire, the work of perhaps dozens of unknown men, women and children was needed.

The Anglo-Saxon period of English history is of immense importance in the story of the nation. From small beginnings on the eastern seaboard of Britain, the English came over several centuries to dominate lowland Britain, and latterly large parts of the globe. During the Anglo-Saxon period the framework of English political systems, law, economic systems, language, literature, social custom, traditions, music and the arts was created.

The Late Saxon, Late Viking & Norman Period

The Late Saxon period, stretching from about AD 950 to AD 1066, was a crucial period of English history. Aside from political developments within the British Isles which would culminate in the kingdoms of Scotland and England, the unified English state took its place in European affairs and became embroiled in the politics of the wider medieval world.

England narrowly avoided becoming a Scandinavian satellite dominated by a Danish ruling class in the early 11th century, only to become a Norman political satellite later in that century. The succeeding Norman period (AD 1054-1066) saw the establishment of some of the most notable buildings in the country – many of the great cathedrals and castles owe their origins to impositions of power and authority by Norman magnates, and even humble village churches often show evidence for their construction in the period AD 1050-1150.

In these pages we will present some of the material evidence for the period – brooches and buckles, stirrup mounts and swords – but the true legacy of the period from AD 1066 to about AD 1150 can be found on every page of every book written in English since then. The Normans had remarkably little effect on English culture, but their dominion affected the English language, the effects of which are still with us today. The language of the nobility was Norman French while that of the rest of the population was English: the Normans used few English words in their speech (other than place-names, river-names and personal names).

The Late Anglo-Saxon period had seen the arrival of Danish settlers, and the absorption by the English of Danish manners and speech. Old English and Old Norse (the language of the Vikings) were not vastly different, sharing many common words with slight differences in pronunciation: the English called a sea-going vessel a *scip* (pronounced 'ship' as it is today), while the Danes called it a *skip*. The English called the tunic worn by men a *sceort* ('shirt') while the Danes called it a *skirt* – and we still retain the words 'shirt' and 'skirt' for our garments. The need to understand each other in daily discourse made simplification of the language necessary: a Dane might say *ek selja hross* and an Englishman *ic selle hors*, both meaning 'I sell [a] horse'. The English evidently became used to mixing their words with Danish idioms and simplifying them to make matters clear. When the Normans arrived, there was little prospect of them learning to speak English, but the English soon learnt Norman words: *chair* instead of *stool* or *settle*, *table* instead of *board*, *plate* instead of *dish* or *bowl*. The English did not stop using their own words, they simply added new words from Norman French to their vocabulary, but the structure of English remained unchanged. An interesting example of this even today is Neil Armstrong's famous phrase: '*One small step for a man, one giant leap for mankind*' in which every word is drawn from the language of the Anglo-Saxons (even 'giant', although ultimately of Greek origin, appears in *Beowulf* and is thoroughly anglicised!). The result is that English has two parallel sets of vocabulary, one for formal occasions and another for informal:

we may enter a room as a guest and receive either a cordial reception or a hearty welcome, two very different sentiments.

The Anglo-Scandinavian and Norman visions for England were very different: the Danes saw England as a great prize, and were keen to settle in the land and take part in Anglo-Saxon society. The Normans, by contrast, seem to have regarded England as a treasure-house to be emptied, taking its wealth back to Normandy to fund yet more expeditions of conquest.

The Physical Evidence

Throughout this book, we shall often differentiate between 'Anglo-Scandinavian' and 'Norman' culture. This may seem an artificial division, since the Anglo-Saxons and Vikings lived on the fringes of the North Sea and the Normans were in origin an expatriate Scandinavian community in north-west France. By complex historical processes – connected in the end to ideas about identity and language – the Normans of the 11th century can no longer be regarded as Scandinavian in anything other than distant origin: their art is Continental European, their language is a regional variant of Old French, their social structure is feudal (like many parts of the former Carolingian Frankish lands) and their architecture owes more to visions of Rome than it does to memories of the fjords. In England, Anglo-Saxon culture and language fused quite happily with contemporary Scandinavian forms into a shared idiom, a common manner of displaying wealth and power, piety and formality. The Norman culture stood firmly outside this tradition, and has to be dealt with separately.

One very obvious way in which the Norman presence can be discerned is in the matter of personal names. The Anglo-Saxon tradition was for a male or female to be given a name composed from two elements, such as *Ead* + *weard* 'blessing + warder', 'one who guards the family's wealth' or *Guþ* + *here* 'war + raider', 'a raiding warrior'. Scandinavian names were formed in the same way: equivalent to *Guþhere* is the Norse *Gunnar*, from *gunn* 'war' (the same word as Old Enginsh *guþ*) and *heri* 'raider' (the same word as Old English *here*). Sometimes Anglo-Saxon and Scandinavian names were shared within families: King Harold Godwineson had brothers called Tostig and Gyrth (Scandinavian names) and Leofwine (a pure Anglo-Saxon

name) as well as Swein which might be from either language. His sister, Edith (Eadgyþ) has an Anglo-Saxon name, while Harold's own name is Scandinavian (Háraldr). The Norman tradition was different: they used regional forms of standard French names such as *Guillelm* (Frankish *Wilhelm* 'protection of willpower') and *Rodbert* (Frankish *Hrodbert* 'bright with glory'), still in use today as William and Robert. They also used biblical names, such as Thomas, John, Stephen and Simeon, and these soon passed into popular usage among the Anglo-Scandinavian population of England.

Anglo-Scandinavian material culture in the 11th century continued the developments of the Middle Saxon period, such as the increased use of pottery and the development of a literate civilisation in which written records were customary and routine. The growth of the church as a commissioner of works of art means that many of the finer surviving pieces from Anglo-Scandinavian England are ecclesiastical in nature.

One new development is an interest in enamel work, especially the champ-levé technique, as a decorative medium; this is probably due to changing political and economic circumstances.

The Scandinavian contribution to Late Anglo-Saxon England is easily overlooked, but it is fair to say that the more vibrant zoomorphic elements of Winchester Style art owe something to contemporary developments in the Ringerike Style. It has been suggested that Scandinavian women in England used contemporary designs, e.g. Borre Style or Ringerike Style, to show their origins (and presumably their Scandinavian loyalties), in just the same way that, centuries earlier, Anglo-Saxon women used their own forms of annular, disc and bow brooch to distance themselves from the Romano-Britons. The continued use of separate styles conveyed a political and social message – and the ultimate merging of these styles into a common Anglo-Scandinavian tradition says much about the political and social ambitions of the users.

Manuscript production flourished in the middle years of the 11th century, and many of the classic Old English texts date from this time – which is to say that the copies which have survived were made then, though the works themselves are much older. Many of the texts were biblical or ecclesiastical – groups of sermons and homilies, for example. But a great many works survive from this period which were not religious in nature: books of medical remedies, for example, treatises on astronomy,

The assimilation of Vikings into Christian Anglo-Saxon England can be seen on this decorated cross shaft at Middleton, Yorkshire, where the wheel-headed cross sits above the figure of a helmetted Viking warrior buried with his shield (top right), sword (below), axe (below his hand), spear (left) and knife (across his midriff)

history, geography, grammar and poetry.

Outside grandiose architecture, no distinctive Norman material culture has ever been identified, in England, on the Continent or in the Near East where Crusader kingdoms were carved out of desert principalities. This may seem surprising – that a people so gifted in warfare and politics should have overlooked the creation of a badge of identity – but it should be borne in mind that the Normans were a recent phenomenon in the 11th century, and had passed into history by the middle of the 12th. While other cultures achieved much in the fields of art and literature in such a short time, there was no such impetus among them. There is the further consideration that the Norman invasion force consisted of many different nationalities (Normans, Flemings, Bretons, etc.), and it may be that there never was a single material or social culture among them.

One of the few artefact types that can be assigned a Norman date with confidence is the later classes of nummular brooch. Nummular brooches were a Middle Saxon innovation: disc brooches decorated in the style of contemporary coins, of which many bear very clear decoration faithfully reproducing the styles of coin then in use. A few examples replicate coins issued by William I and his successors and must therefore date to after 1066.

The introduction of castles into the English landscape is often attributed to the Normans, but there are clear signs in later Anglo-Saxon England that fortifications of a similar type were already being built in the mid-11th century – possibly by Anglo-Saxons influenced by developments on the Continent. That said, castles were used widely by the Norman aristocracy as a means of reminding the populace that the land was no longer under their control – an example of architecture expressing a relationship of dominance.

There are two exceptional records of England in the Norman period – one pictorial, the other literary - which combine to throw light on many aspects of life in those times. One is the Bayeux Tapestry, which is in fact an embroidered wall-hanging (not a woven tapestry), allegedly commissioned by Bishop Odo of Bayeux, the half-brother of William I, sometime Earl of Kent. See section 2.1 for details.

The other major record of William's reign is the *Domesdæg* or 'Doomsday [Survey]', recorded in two volumes and now held by the Public Record Office. The survey was undertaken at William's command in 1086 in order to find out for sure exactly what wealth there was in England, and how much of it belonged to the king. The *Laud manuscript* of the *Anglo-Saxon Chronicle* (s.a. 1085) shows how the people of England viewed this enterprise:

Then he sent his men all over England into every shire to discover how many hundred hides of land there were in that shire, and what land and livestock the king himself owned in that land, and what dues he should have from that shire in [every] twelve months. He also had written out how much land his archbishops had, and his diocesan bishops, and his abbots and his earls, and - though I tell it too long - what or how much each man owned who was a landholder in England in land or in livestock, and how much money it was worth. So very thoroughly did he have the survey made that there was not a single hide, nor one yard of land, nor even – it is shameful to tell [of it] but it did not seem to him shameful to do – one ox, nor one cow, nor one pig was left which was not set down in his writings.

(A hide of land is a plot sufficient to support one family; its dimensions would vary according to the quality of the soil.) The writings were collected into two volumes: the *Great Doomsday Book*, probably written at the king's chancery in Winchester, covering all of England except Durham and Northumberland and the area covered by the *Little Doomsday Book* – Essex, Suffolk and Norfolk. Parts of Wales were included in the survey, but the northern counties and the great cities of London and Winchester were not, probably for administrative reasons. The records give the names of landholders in each county and the places they held, their current (1086) value and often their value in the time of King Edward the Confessor, what assets were there (livestock, arable land, watermills and so on), the numbers of fee-paying tenants and the tax assessment.

The survey is a unique document in Europe at this time, and is a testament to the Late Saxon chancery which already had the ability to collect data on this scale and to turn it into an assessment for taxation. The thoroughness of the royal survey clearly astonished the *Chronicle's* writer, but William must have been aware that his English scribes and inquisitors were capable of gathering the information. The *Great Doomsday* was written out by one man (with notes supplied in another hand), while at least six men worked on the *Little Doomsday* – suggesting that the book was compiled in East Anglia or Essex by the commissioners who gathered the information. The *ASC* tells us that William had the idea for the survey over Christmas 1085, work began in 1086 and was almost complete at the time of William's death in September 1087; it may be that the king's death occurred before work on the Essex, Suffolk and Norfolk entries had been completed and these records were bound separately.

One unintended benefit of the *Domesdæg* survey was that the names of many (more than thirteen thousand) English and Welsh towns and villages are recorded for the first time in its pages. This has made the study of early English place-names possible on a vast scale.

The Normans systematically emptied English churches of their great treasures, and shipped them off to enrich their own holdings on the Continent. It is for this reason that many high-status Anglo-Saxon objects have been found outside England: the Franks casket, the Gandersheim casket, the Tassilo chalice and many others.

A further consequence of the Norman invasion is the effect it had on English literature. Having no valid claim to settle in England, the Norman reaction to this morally precarious position was to attempt to undermine the basis for the Anglo-Saxons' title to the land. They did this through promotion of an obscure set of Welsh tales which dealt with the adventures of a legendary king and his circle of heroic companions: in the hands of Norman and later storytellers, these rather mysterious tales became the Arthurian legends which inspired artists throughout the Middle Ages.

The End of Anglo-Saxon England

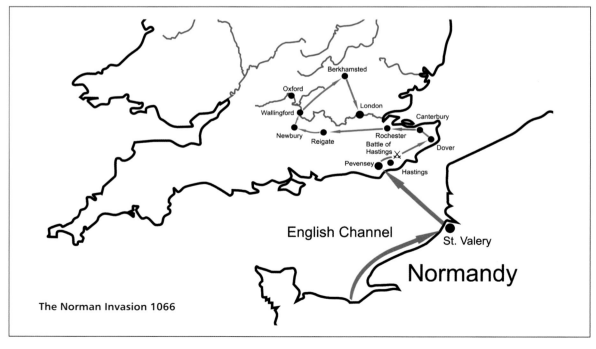

The Norman Invasion 1066

Outline of Late Saxon & Norman England (AD 950-1150)

The history of Late Saxon England can best be described as 'turbulent'. It is perfectly possible that the preceding centuries were every bit as turbulent as the years 950 to 1066, but the fact is that this period is better documented than almost any previous period of northern European history, and our understanding of the people and events is therefore more rounded and can be set into a fuller context. The century of Norman rule (1066-1154) was likewise characterised by a gross centralisation of power, such as no Anglo-Saxon ruler had ever been able to attempt. In many ways, the Late Anglo-Saxon state was so easily toppled precisely because it was such an efficient mechanism for governance: the incoming ruler had only to seize the levers of power in order to take control.

After the unification of England into a single state, achieved by King Athelstan and defended by his armies at the battle of *Brunanburh* in AD 937, there followed a succession of short-lived kings: Eadmund (939-946), Eadred (946-955), Eadwig (955-959), Edgar the Peaceable (959-975) and Edward the Martyr (975-978). During this period, power was consolidated into the hands of *ealdormenn* (regional governors) who administered their regions as delegates of the king; many of these regions were former kingdoms, such as East Anglia and Mercia. The previous Kingdom of York, which Athelstan had tried to subjugate, proved a very difficult problem: the rulers of the kingdom were sponsored by the Dublin Vikings and considered the territory to be part of the Scandinavian world, while the Anglo-Saxon kings in Winchester regarded it as part of their natural domain. This tension between Winchester and Dublin entailed several rapid changes of leader in York, as various factions tried to ensure that their favoured warlord ruled that kingdom. By AD 954, a weakened York was absorbed into the English state as an earldom, but local sympathies were still strongly Scandinavian among some elements of the population who feared loss of independence.

King Edward the Martyr

King Edward the Martyr was treacherously murdered at Corfe in AD 978, having ruled for just three years, during which time there was a power-struggle between supporters of Edward, aged thirteen when he came to the throne, and his younger half-brother Æthelred. It is likely that powerful magnates saw the accession of the young king as an opportunity to gain more wealth and influence at court; at the same time, a religious reform was underway, promoted by Edward's father King Edgar, which offered opportunities to leading clerics to improve their positions. Factionalism and bitter rivalries at court among the secular and ecclesiastical magnates led to dangerous rifts, and England was close to breaking apart in civil war. The king himself was petulant and hot-headed, and offended many of the leading men with his behaviour; he was also nearing the age at which he would no longer be dominated by his mother or his courtiers. In this volatile climate, the murder of the young king in front of his mother and half-brother offered a perfect opportunity to demonstrate to the successor, his half-brother Æthelred, the likely consequences of making enemies among the earls. Edward was hailed as a martyr by some churchmen, suggesting that there was a religious dimension to his murder, but it is more likely that the story of martyrdom was a political move by those who lost out through his death.

King Æthelred

Edward's younger half-brother, Æthelred, came to the throne, at the age of about ten. The king relied on his Witan, the council of 'wise men' who advised an Anglo-Saxon king, drawn from the ranks of the clergy and most powerful landowners. With the consolidation of territory and power into the hands of a few, very powerful magnates, the political rivalries among the Witan led inevitably to poor decision-making. A strong king would have controlled his advisers, but Æthelred was a boy who had recently seen his own brother murdered - probably by agents of the men who were supposed to assist him. Gifts of land made by his father, King Edgar, to found ecclesiastical houses were taken back by the *ealdormenn* in whose territories they stood.

Perhaps sensing weakness in the English leadership, Danish raiding resumed from about AD 980; there had been no effective Viking activity in England since the days of Edward the Elder, but the accession of the boy-king was an opportunity for plunder. In AD 991 a large Viking fleet assembled and ravaged the coasts of southern and eastern England. After sacking Ipswich, the raiders set up camp on an island in the River Blackwater in Essex, below the mint-town of Maldon. The local earl, Byrhtnoth, decided that the Vikings had to be stopped while they were stationary, and summoned his forces to attack them. The island on which they were camped was accessible by a narrow causeway, and the English commander set three warriors to guard this, killing any Vikings who tried to cross. The Viking leader, who may have been Ólaf Tryggvason, later king of Norway, sent a messenger asking for a payment of money in return for which the fleet would leave, but Byrhtnoth scorned this offer and told him that the points of spears and blades of swords would be the only payment the Vikings could expect from him. In the negotiations which followed, the Vikings asked for permission to cross the causeway to settle the matter, and the English commander agreed. In the ensuing battle, Byrhtnoth was cut down and, seeing this, some of the English troops fled but the ealdorman's own warriors, his *heorðgeneatas* or hearth-companions, stayed and fought on around his body until they were all killed. This encounter is the subject of a famous poem, *The Battle of Maldon*, one of the finest examples of late Old English verse. According to later legend, the Vikings took Byrhtnoth's head with them when they sailed for London, where they demanded even more money in return for their departure. King Æthelred was indecisive but some loud voices among the Witan suggested that buying peace was the best answer in the short term – even King Alfred had needed to do this. A *Denegeld* (Danegeld, payment to the Danes) of £22,000 was agreed, the first of many such payments which Æthelred had to make, funded by heavy taxes on English commerce and land. The king stood sponsor to Ólaf at his baptism in AD 994 and their agreement stipulated that Ólaf should never return to England with hostile intent; for Ólaf's part, he seems to have honoured the bargain, and returned to Norway where he set about forcing the population to become Christian, often using violent and oppressive means to achieve this. Because Viking fleets comprised an aggregation of individual leaders, each with several ships under his command, it is likely that many of the Vikings remained in England despite the agreement which their leader had made.

King Sven Forkbeard

The Viking menace did not disappear: the promise of easy money attracted more Vikings, whose demands grew ever larger. The church at this time had been preaching sermons about the return of Christ in the year AD 1000 and the punishments he would bring, and the times were characterised by fear and instability. Æthelred, badly advised as ever, issued one of the most disastrous proclamations: in AD 1002 he ordered the massacre of all Danes in England on St. Brice's day (13th November). It is unclear to what extent the order was carried out, but it is likely that in some parts of the country where the Danes were few it was executed, while elsewhere the Danes were too numerous for it to be attempted. One of the victims was a Danish lady, Gunnhild, the sister of Sven Forkbeard, heir to the Danish throne; her murder may have prompted Sven's reprisals in AD 1004. Sven's forces were halted and perhaps destroyed in East Anglia, in battle at Thetford in AD 1005, and he returned to Denmark to recruit a new force. Back in England in AD 1007, Sven took a larger tribute than ever paid before at £36,000. Æthelred gambled on a new English fleet to counter the

Danish menace but in the event, one of the naval commanders fell out with the Witan and took his ships on a freebooting mission.

By AD 1013, financed by his raids on England, Sven felt himself strong enough to raise the stakes: he led a larger force than ever with the intention of making himself king. The English resistance to the Vikings collapsed under weak leadership and the king earnt his nickname, Ethelred the Unready. (The name Æthelred means 'noble advice', but his nickname *unræd* means either 'no advice' or 'bad advice' – both very appropriate for this monarch.) Æthelred took the only course open to him: already married to a Norman princess, he fled to exile in Normandy and Sven became effective ruler of England.

King Cnut

Sven's success was short-lived: in February AD 1014 he died, and his forces fragmented. Some immediately accepted his son, Cnut, as their leader, but the English Witan sent for Æthelred to return and lead them as long as he would be a true lord and forgive all the actions they had taken against him. (This is the first recorded example in English history of a king being forced to accept terms dictated by his subjects.) The English leaders took the offensive and moved against Cnut's forces; the young Dane, perhaps unsure whether he could command the support of his father's allies, foresaw defeat and fled to Denmark leaving many of his father's men and his supporters in Lindsey (the northern part of Lincolnshire, formerly an Anglo-Saxon kingdom) to the revenge of the English troops.

The Danes' devastation of Lindsey led to a great deal of bitterness and increased support for Æthelred's son, Edmund Ironside, in preference to either Æthelred or Cnut. In AD 1015 Cnut returned, determined to finish his father's project of acquiring the throne of England; English resistance focused on Edmund, who proved himself a capable and determined warrior; Æthelred died in April AD 1016 and the fight against the Danes fell to his son. Despite many indecisive encounters between Viking and English forces, Edmund constantly managed to rally new troops to his banner and to deny Cnut the throne. In October AD 1016, Cnut and Edmund met at Ashingdon, Essex; Edmund's army proved the stronger and the day appeared to be his, but one of the English commanders, Eadric Streona (Æthelred's son-in-law) with his forces from the West Midlands, feigned illness and withdrew, leaving Edmund's troops weakened. It is likely that Eadric was in league

King Cnut presents a cross to the cathedral at Winchester (from the Stowe Manuscript)

with Cnut, and saw political advantage in throwing victory to the Dane. The strife came to an end when the two leaders agreed to divide the land between them, with Cnut holding all the country outside Wessex (i.e. the lands south of the Thames) and Edmund holding the Wessex territory; the agreement lasted only a few months as Edmund died mysteriously later the same year and Cnut became the sole ruler.

On his accession, Cnut proved himself a very capable ruler. He married Æthelred's widow, Emma, in order to establish legitimacy for his reign. He quickly dealt with traitors such as Eadric Streona and Thorkel the Tall (a Danish general who had supported Æthelred and Edmund Ironside), collected a larger Danegeld than ever with which with he paid off his mercenary troops and re-organised the English shires into a simpler and more efficient system under men he believed he could trust, one of whom was a Sussex nobleman called Godwine who took control of Wessex. This Earl Godwine rose to a position of immense power under Cnut's regime, and soon became second only to the king and church in wealth and authority. Cnut maintained his own troops – a fleet of forty ships with their crews – which he used as a standing army. There is little doubt that Cnut dealt with potential rivals harshly, tolerated no resistance to his authority and perhaps organised the mysterious deaths of several people he could not defeat militarily. He certainly acted vigorously to defend his territories from raiding, and put down any attempt to usurp power.

Cnut Svensson (known in older history books as 'King Canute') became king of England, yet through his father he had a strong claim to the Danish throne which he enforced on his return to Denmark in AD 1018. Despite his early career as an opportunistic Viking, Cnut had considerable foresight and was able to draw on the talents of both Danes and Englishmen to rule his 'North Sea empire', which he expanded in AD 1028 with his claim to kingship in Norway and his dominance of some of the cities of Sweden. Cnut's rise to power checked the dominance of the Hiberno-Norse in Dublin and finished any hope of re-establishing the Viking Kingdom of York; rulers of principalities in Wales, Scotland and Ireland accepted him as their overlord. As the ruler of Christian England, Cnut saw the benefits of an orderly state and tried to bring Denmark further into the orbit of European monarchies, dealing with the Pope as the king of several large countries. Cnut used the craftsmanship of English workshops to make prestigious gifts across the European political scene, winning him glory and allies. He issued a law-code in the Anglo-Saxon manner, upheld the position and power of the church, journeyed to Rome for a papal blessing, encouraged record-keeping and religious observance, reformed the coinage and generally did everything expected of a medieval European monarch.

Kings Harthacnut, Harold I & Edward the Confessor

Cnut's death in AD 1035 led to a succession crisis: in Denmark, his son Harthacnut was already acting as regent (King Cnut III) and fortified his position there in a war against King Magnus I of Norway, but his pre-occupation with Scandinavian affairs lost him any support he might have had in England. Another son, Harold I (Harold Harefoot), reigned in England but his early death in AD 1040 left the English throne vacant; Æthelred's sons, Edward and Alfred, attempted to stake their claims to rule in England, but they failed to gain the support of the leading men. Edward escaped back to Normandy, but Alfred was captured by Earl Godwin of Wessex, who handed him over to Harold Harefoot. The king had him blinded and he died soon after.

Harthacnut won peace in Scandinavia in order to come to England and claim his father's inheritance, but the re-union of England and Denmark lasted only two years until Harthacnut himself died. At this point, Danish unity fell apart amid rivalry between King Magnus I of Norway and a local claimant, Sven Estridsson. Magnus's death in AD 1047 allowed Danish suzerainty to be re-imposed, but the entitlement to the English throne was lost. Harthacnut had made a treaty with Æthelred's son, Edward, to return from exile in Normandy and rule in England; if either died without an heir, both thrones, English and Danish, would go to the other. Edward's half-brother, Edmund Ironside, had died after making his treaty with Cnut, and Edward was left as the only claimant to the kingship of England, and with him came many Normans whom he installed in positions of power on his return in AD 1041.

The Normans had given their name to Normandy, a region of north-western France previously called Armorica. Their nobles believed themselves to be descended from Viking settlers who were awarded lands by the king of Francia in return for keeping it secure from attack. The majority of the population of Normandy was probably Frankish (or ultimately Gallo-Roman) and their group identity emerged in the early 10th century, and gradually became an autonomous duchy or state with only nominal ties to the crown of Francia. The name is based on the term *Nortmanni* (Northmen), referring to the Norwegian founder, Rollo (i.e. Hrolfr).

From its earliest history, the Norman state was highly militarised in character and displayed this through lavish military equipment. Norman nobles, when not engaged in war, practised for it by hawking and hunting. Norman leaders were quick to make alliances with powerful neighbours, to recruit skilled men to their retinues and to marry into wealthy families to secure their possessions: in this they were not very different from Anglo-Saxon and Scandinavian rulers of the period. Normandy was never a kingdom but retained a feudal submission to Francia; its only opportunity to further its aims was to intervene in the affairs of neighbours.

Edward had grown up in Normandy from the age of about thirteen and evidently had an agreeable lifestyle there at the court, with the status of an exiled prince who had little prospect of returning to his homeland. Edward enjoyed close ties to the Norman nobles, as his mother, Emma, was from a prominent family, being the daughter of Richard, Duke of Normandy. (Emma had been married to both

King Edward the Confessor enthroned on the Bayeux Tapestry

King Æthelred and King Cnut successively.) His unsuccessful attempt on the English throne, which led to his brother's death, caused very bad relations between the king and his most prominent subject, Earl Godwine of Wessex, whom Edward probably blamed for the torture of his brother, Alfred. Two other powerful men were also building their own powerbases: Leofric, earl of Mercia and Siward, earl of Northumbria. Earl Godwine had been a particular favourite of King Cnut, and had supported Harthacnut during his short reign. Godwine had made an astute marriage to a lady named Gytha, who seems to have been a member of a leading Danish family and perhaps a relative of Cnut himself. The couple's children bore a mix of English, Danish and Anglo-Scandinavian names: Swegen (or Sven, Swein), Harold, Tostig, Edith, Gyrth, Gunnhild, Ælfgifu, Leofwine and Wulfnoth.

Edward's reign was militarily uneventful in as much as no immediate threat of invasion faced England; his religious piety earnt him the soubriquet 'the Confessor'. Border wars with the Scots and Welsh continued, as they had for generations, and trouble in Scandinavia still threatened to embroil English leaders. Edward had to find a settlement which would provide him with the support of Earls Godwine, Leofric and Siward. In order to mollify Godwine and the Wessex thanes, the king agreed to marry Godwine's daughter, Edith; no children are known to have issued from this union, leading scholars to speculate that it it may have been nothing more than a manoeuvre on the king's part to buy Godwine's acquiescence. Edward's insistence on supporting Norman favourites at court, and the general hostility which they met with from the Anglo-Scandinavian nobility,

caused immense friction. Earl Godwine led the opposition to *þa frenciscan men* 'those Frankish men' as the *ASC* calls them, and matters came to a head when the appointment of a new archbishop of Canterbury had to be made: Godwine supported the Anglo-Saxon Æthelric but Edward appointed the Norman cleric, Robert of Jumièges. Riots took place in Dover against the rule of Eustace, count of Boulogne, who was another Norman imposed by Edward; Earl Godwine was responsible for public order, but refused to punish the townsfolk. Earls Leofric and Siward sided with the king against Godwine, and in AD 1051 the whole family was sent into exile, even Queen Edith who was confined to a nunnery at Wherwell in Hampshire.

Within a year, Godwine and his formidable sons were back with the support of a military force and the king had to back down, reinstate Godwine to the rank of earl and restore all his territories to him. Edward's position was severely weakened by this humiliating reversal, and he was forced to send his Norman favourites back to Normandy. For the next decade Godwine and his leading son, Harold, extended their power, securing leadership of all the earldoms except Mercia by AD 1057. Godwine died in AD 1053, leaving the Godwinesons the most powerful family in England, and Harold himself took control of negotiations with the Welsh following punitive expeditions which he led in AD 1063, and dealt with secession in Northumbria in AD 1065. Harold was in every respect acting as if he were the king of England, and when Edward died in January 1066, he rectified the situation by being proclaimed king.

King Harold II

This development did not go unnoticed in Normandy or in Scandinavia. The Norman Duke, William the Bastard, the illegitimate son of Duke Robert, claimed that Edward had awarded him the throne of England if he should die without an heir, and that Harold had been sent to Normandy towards the end of Edward's life to formalise this arrangement. Even Norman sources agree that, on his deathbed, Edward appointed Harold as his heir. In Anglo-Saxon tradition, the succession of kingship did not automatically pass from father to son: kings were drawn from among the eligible males of the royal family, and often had to fend off the claims of rivals; in that sense, the crown of England was not in Edward's gift in the first place. The Wessex royal line included a few surviving minor figures, none of whom had any support among the earls. Duke William, no longer content with the vassal status implied by his title, took steps to secure the throne of England.

Harold Godwinesson with a spear in the prow of his ship, on the Bayeux Tapestry

At the same time, a Viking adventurer named Hárald Sigurðsson *Harðráða* (hard-counsel) who came to the throne of Norway in AD 1047, entered the fray. Hárald had been exiled in his youth and spent most of his adult life fighting in the Varangian guard, the élite bodyguard of the Roman Emperors in Constantinople. Returning home with considerable wealth and a reputation for ferocity and cunning, Hárald set about regaining Denmark; along with his claim to the Danish throne, Hárald felt that he had a parallel claim on that of England due to the union of the two countries under King Cnut and his son, Harthacnut. Norwegian support for Hárald was weak, but there was no effective opposition and he imposed his authority at sword-point throughout the land. A treaty was made between Hárald and the Danish leader, Svein, which allowed the king to abandon his fruitless attempt at political union between Norway and Denmark, and freed Hárald for another enterprise – the invasion of England.

AD 1066

The earldom of Northumbria, on the death of Siward in AD 1055, was awarded to Tostig Godwinesson, the younger brother of Harold, who married Judith, daughter of Count Baldwin IV of Flanders. Tostig's career as an earl was not glorious: he alienated the Anglo-Scandinavian country folk and punished opposition among the leading families violently. His family ties in Wessex meant he was frequently away at the Winchester court, and he probably failed to deal effectively with the perennial problem of Scottish border-raids. In AD 1065, Northumbrian thanes rose against Tostig and drove his officers out of York; Edward sent Harold to negotiate with the Northumbrians, and he realised that Tostig could not resume his office without risking more trouble. Harold asked Edward to banish Tostig, to which the elderly king agreed, but through this the brothers' rivalry was exacerbated and Tostig determined to gain vengeance. He sailed to his wife's family in Flanders and was provided with a fleet by Count Baldwin; Tostig attempted an invasion in May 1066 but succeeded only in forcing his brothers to unite against him. The rest of the summer Tostig spent in Scotland, where he hatched a plan to persuade Hárald Harðráða to assist him with an invasion of Northumbria.

King Harold II at his coronation by Archbishop Stigand, with his followers in attendance, from the Bayeux Tapestry

By late summer of 1066, three very able military commanders faced each other across the seas surrounding England's eastern and southern shores: Harold Godwinesson, aged about 44, proclaimed King of England and an exceptional leader and fighting man; Hárald Harðráða, aged about 51, the veteran of nearly four decades of warfare; William of Normandy, aged about 38, determined to break free of the confines of his land's feudal ties to the throne of France. After the failure of Tostig's desperate attempt to persuade his brother Gyrth, Earl of East Anglia, to join the resistance to Harold, the scene was set for yet more desperate encounters.

Harold Godwinesson knew that he should expect an attack, either from Hárald or from William, during the summer of 1066; troops were mobilised and stood ready but as the summer drew on, no sign appeared of an invasion force. By harvest time, invasion seemed less likely, and the army was partly stood down; Harold's fleet was recalled to London. In September, very late in the year for any such attack, Hárald of Norway sailed for England on the advice of Tostig, who had probably promised the Norwegian the support of the northern shires if he could make landfall and overcome Harold's earls. The fleet is believed to have numbered about 300 ships, with about 15,000 men – Norwegians but also Icelanders and other Scandinavians, and the disaffected Englishmen who followed Tostig. Hárald landed in the River Humber and engaged the northern earls at Fulford Gate near York, where he gained a swift victory. Believing that he could expect the imminent surrender of the rest of the land, Hárald sent out foraging parties to collect 'tribute' while the bulk of his army stayed with the ships. King Harold was of course aware of the landing and marched his army north with great speed, coming on Hárald's men on 25th September at Stamford Bridge. The Vikings were lightly armed and taken by surprise, while Harold's men were prepared for war. By the end of that day, King Hárald of Norway lay among the slain and there were only enough Norwegians left alive to man 24 of their ships for the return journey.

With the death of Hárald of Norway, the Viking age came to an end. Internal political rivalries, forced Christian conversion and the bloody and complex process of state-formation was already underway, which meant that the energies of the Scandinavian ruling classes were focussed inwards. While Danish kings continued to play a part in the politics of England, and those of Norway in Scotland, they were never more than participants and no longer dominated the political scene.

Harold's victory was total, the Norwegian claim to England was thwarted, but there was no cause for celebration. Within days, the Normans arrived on the south coast and began erecting a fortification on the cliffs above the port of Hastings, from which they could protect their supply lines. William's men were supplemented by mercenaries, including Breton archers. The Norman cavalry for which William's army was famed, were also present. William had secured the blessing of Pope Alexander II for his mission, and had a consecrated banner with him from the papal office.

Duke William of Normandy with his half-brother (to his right), Bishop Odo, from the Bayeux Tapestry

Harold brought his victorious army from Yorkshire to the South Downs in an attempt to pen the Normans in the Hastings area. Meanwhile, William began sending his forces northwards towards London. The two armies collided at a place called *Sandlagu* 'sand-lake', which the Normans later renamed *Senlac* 'lake of blood'. The battle which took place on the slopes of Senlac hill turned the tide of English history: Harold, the last English king of England, fell in the battle with his brothers and many of his men; William the Bastard, the invader, seized power and was renamed William the Conqueror; the majority of the English nobility who survived the battle were dispossessed of their lands and titles.

Because late Anglo-Saxon England was a well-run state with the means of collecting taxes and delivering justice, the removal and replacement of the king and leading men caused little disruption initially: life went on as before for farmers and fishermen.

King William I

William marched on London and demanded to be crowned king of England (map page 12); the Witan initially refused and adopted the young Edgar as king. William's forces were beaten back from London, and had to march westward around the city; a second attempt to enter London succeeded once Stigand, the archbishop, had withdrawn support from Edgar. William was crowned on Christmas Day AD 1066 in Westminster Abbey. Resistance to William did not collapse immediately – in areas such as the fens of East Anglia, in the Welsh Marches and in some of the northern shires rebellions were staged and a Danish invasion was even attempted, but William dealt with all these threats with characteristic ruthlessness. William ordered the devastation of the north – whereby whole villages were destroyed, the people turned out into the roads, their crops burnt, their houses torched, their cattle slaughtered, their tools broken. As much as a century later there were still estates which had not recovered from William's 'Harrying of the North'. The ravaging was so fierce that William lost papal support, but after ten years of governance in England he no longer perceived any further threats to his power. It is estimated that the English élite had been all but eradicated within four years of his arrival; many of the warrior class joined the Varangian guard in Constantinople. English estates were handed out to William's favourites, but he seems to have had a policy of keeping the parcels of land separate so that no single landowner could gain wide support in any county.

Duke William lifts his helmet to show his men that he is still alive at a crucial moment in the battle. In the lower margin, a troop of archers moves forward.

William's men were obliged to govern from positions of power and military strength because they did not have the active support of the subject population. This led to the construction of castles at strategic points, from which armed cavalry could suppress insurrection and enforce Norman law. William's men spoke Norman French – a regional dialect – which became the language of the courts and of governance. William's English-speaking subjects were effectively excluded from the processes of the law unless they could persuade a Norman to assist them.

Towards the end of his reign, William began to take stock of the country he had won and decided to make a definitive survey so that he could exact as much tax as possible from it; this is the origin of the *Domesdæg Book* (see page 11).

William's natural ambitiousness was evident and the French king, Philip I, determined to rein in his vassal duke, but internal rivalries within France and Normandy meant that the two states were always on the verge of war, even if it was never formally declared. William's half-brother, Bishop Odo of Bayeux, caused further outrage and was stripped of his possessions in England but retained clerical office.

In AD 1087, William was campaigning in France, burning the town of Mantes, near Paris, when he fell off his horse, suffering internal injuries in the process. Suspecting that his end was near, the king divided his lands among his surviving sons, with England falling to William Rufus. His eldest son, Robert, received Normandy, and the youngest, Henry, received a grant of money with which to buy land. His daughters were betrothed to leading men from many European states.

William was buried at Caen, Normandy in September AD 1087. In an absurd and rather grotesque final tableau, due to the heat William's body had swollen and would not fit into the stone sarcophagus constructed for his burial, obliging the attending bishops to force the corpse into the container; the king's abdomen burst, filling the coffin with its putrefied contents and leaving a foul smell in the church.

King William II

Norman domination of England did not end with William's death, as William II (William Rufus) came to the throne at the age of thirty-one and continued his father's policies of oppression and military force. He also managed to alienate the church, and therefore suffered from a very bad press during his life, including veiled references to sexual irregularity: he remained unmarried, produced no known offspring and preferred the company of men such as Ranulf Flambard, his favoured minister whom he made bishop of Durham. William II was always under the shadow of his elder brother, Robert Curthose, who inherited Normandy; both men joined forces to counter the manoeuvring of their younger sibling, Henry. Although William II generally despised the English, he came increasingly to rely on the support of Norman barons in England against Robert's influence. In AD 1091, William II invaded Normandy and seized lands from his brother; the pair then set about taking Maine from the kingdom of France.

Only with difficulty could William II keep his Norman barons from destroying each other in vicious power struggles. He quelled the Scots under King Malcolm III, and seized the land of Cumbria which he subdued with the building of Carlisle castle, but had little luck in dealing with the Welsh despite military expeditions in AD 1096 and 1097. William used the English taxation system to raise a large sum of money, which he lent to his brother Robert to finance his participation in the First Crusade; in return, William became regent in Normandy during Robert's absence and pursued campaigns of conquest in the Maine region.

William met his death in AD 1100 while hunting in the New Forest: an arrow pierced his chest, killing him outright, and his Norman companions, fearing that Norman privilege might end with his death, left his body where it fell in order to return to their estates and secure them. William's younger brother, Henry, raced to Winchester to secure the treasury, and from there to London for a hasty coronation as Henry I. The bowman who killed William was his friend, Walter Tyrrell; despite much later speculation that the shot was intentional, an unfortunate accident is the most likely explanation. There were many in the church who had suffered at William's hands and saw in this ignominious end the hand of God acting to rid the land of an unscrupulous tyrant.

King Henry I

Henry I was crowned in AD 1100; his nickname is *Beauclerc* (good clerk) because of his scholarly leanings. Henry would probably not have managed to secure the crown of England had his brother, Robert, not been away on the First Crusade. On Robert's return in AD 1101, the Norman duke attempted an invasion of England, but the re-conquest resulted in a negotiated settlement whereby Henry paid his brother an annual fee in return for his acquiescence. Henry had already married Edith, the daughter of King Malcolm III of Scotland, and perhaps had the support of the English population to a greater degree than his father or brother: Edith was from the house of Wessex, and was the great-granddaughter of Edmund Ironside.

Not content to fill the coffers of England, Henry led an expeditionary force against Normandy on 28th September 1106 – forty years after his father, William, had left Normandy under arms for England. Robert

drove his men north to meet Henry's forces and the two armies unexpectedly collided at Tinchebray; the resultant battle was chaotic, but by evening Robert's bungled attempt at retreat resulted in his capture by Henry's men. Robert was held prisoner in England while Henry reunited his father's holdings on both sides of the Channel; significantly, Henry eschewed the title of Duke of Normandy and preferred King of England.

Henry I holds the record for the largest number of illegitimate children born to a single English king, numbering between twenty and twenty-five according to contemporary sources.

King Stephen, Empress Matilda & the Anarchy

In AD 1135, while in Normandy on state and family business, Henry succumbed to food poisoning and died on 1st December aged about sixty-six. His remains were transported to England and buried at Reading Abbey, a recent foundation of his. Henry's leading nobles had sworn to support the claim of his daughter, Empress Matilda, to the throne but in the event her marriage into the House of Anjou – the leading rivals of the Norman dynasty – persuaded some of them to abandon her cause; Henry's nephew, Stephen of Blois, arrived in England to pursue his claim with the support of some of the barons. The civil strife caused by the feuding between these two factions resulted in Stephen's reign being known as the 'Anarchy' i.e. a society without any leader. Stephen was one of ten children, nearly all of whom held important positions, and had been brought up at his uncle's court from the age of about ten years old. Confusingly, his wife was also known as Matilda; she became Countess of Boulogne in about AD 1125, making Stephen the Count by marriage.

Empress Matilda's marriage to Geoffrey of Anjou cost her the support of the Anglo-Norman barons, and Stephen capitalised on her weakness to seize power, backed by Pope Innocent II. Campaigns against the Welsh and King David I of Scotland occupied the early years of his reign, but his popularity waned and Empress Matilda – supported by a few ambitious barons – took the initiative. Several battles ensued, with King Stephen captured and imprisoned, then released in exchange for the Earl of Gloucester, Empress Matilda's half-brother. A Norman military intervention led by Henry, Empress Matilda's son, almost finished

Stephen, but a series of defeats and lack of funds forced Henry to reconsider: he accepted King Stephen's offer of help in return for his support, and in AD 1153 terms were arranged between Stephen, Empress Matilda and Henry whereby Stephen would reign for the rest of his life, to be succeeded by Henry, Empress Matilda's son.

The *Laud manuscript* of the *ASC* has this to say about King Stephen's reign and the tyranny of the Norman barons:

When the traitors saw that he [Stephen] was a gentle man, kindly and good[-hearted] and did no justice [i.e. did not bring them to justice], then they committed all wonders...For every wealthy man built himself castles and held them against [the king]; and they filled the land full of castles. They severely burdened the wretched men of the land with castle-work [forced labour on castles]; when the castles were built, they filled them with devils and evil men. Then they seized those people whom they thought to have any goods, both by night and by day, men and women, and put them into prison for their gold and silver, and tormented them with unspeakable tortures.

Stephen lived just a few more months, dying at Dover in AD 1154. With his passing, the Norman dynasty ended in England, and the House of Anjou came to power.

The Normans went on to have many adventures in the Mediterranean, and were among the prime movers in the Crusades, but their hold over England ebbed and their nine decades of rule ended ignominiously in civil war. In that time, England became embroiled in costly and ultimately futile religious wars – the Crusades - and the lot of the lower ranks greatly deteriorated: no man under the feudal system, was truly free, since he owed his position to a superior; no woman could own property outright, only through a male relative.

Script

While there are occasional examples of runic script from Late Saxon England, such as the tombstone from St. Paul's churchyard, London, it is fairly safe to say that runes were no longer a major means of communication in England by the 11th century. A few manuscripts show that they were not entirely forgotten, but they had become an antiquarian diversion for clerics rather than a practical script. There are examples of Scandinavian runes on objects from the 10th-11th centuries which may have been made in Denmark or Norway, and found their way to England with their owners.

Later Anglo-Saxon manuscripts were written in a formal script called the English or Winchester bookhand, which is so neat and uses so few abbreviations that it can be transliterated from the manuscript almost without alteration. (Although the script was despised by Norman scribes and abandoned, its clarity and formal beauty recommended it to William Morris who adapted it to his Foundation Hand, which forms the basis for modern English handwriting.)

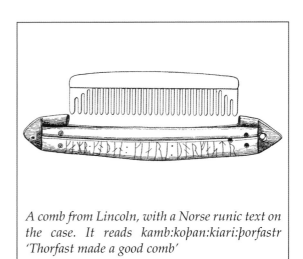

A comb from Lincoln, with a Norse runic text on the case. It reads kamb:koþan:kiari:þorfastr 'Thorfast made a good comb'

Norman scribes used a derived form of Carolingian script for their documents, and dispensed with the Anglo-Saxon letters þ, ƿ ,æ, ȝ and ð (using th, w, a, y and th respectively). Unfortunately, the simplified alphabet they used could not cope with the sounds of English, so that Rotherham was reduced to *Rodreham*, and Sherington is *Serintone*.

Artefact Production & Distribution

The Middle Saxon period had seen the move to planned economic bases and fixed production sites; during the Later Saxon period this concentration of manpower into specialist production sites continued. Important early markets such as Southampton, London, Ipswich and York continued to dominate their territories due to the access to navigable waterways they enjoyed, but new centres emerged as the patterns of commerce changed over the centuries. With Æthelstan's conquest of the Danelaw and creation of a single kingdom of England, even the smallest and most isolated regional communities had contact with men from the peripheries of the kingdom (see maps pages 24, 110). The effect on material culture was a trend towards standardisation, to make certain styles into badges of identity.

By the Anglo-Scandinavian period, with increased Danish influence and a unified Anglo-Saxon state, some items become almost homogenised: a lozenge-shaped stirrup mount might have been used in Yorkshire or Devon and there is nothing in its decoration or manufacture to indicate which. (While there are apparent regional preferences in stirrup mount styles, this is partly due to greater metal-detecting activity in some areas: a more complete catalogue of finds than was available to Williams in his 1997 study would certainly show less markedly regional patterns.)

The generally more homogeneous nature of Anglo-Scandinavian artefacts – be they swords, brooches, buckles or tools – implies an interchange of ideas across a wider area, and the development of regional and even national standard forms of manufacture. While the humble village blacksmith continued to produce knives, chisels, saws, gouges and similar small items, the range of models he was able to work from evidently narrowed to a few, highly developed forms.

The design and production of church artefacts continued to be a unifying factor across the country, although the taste of the leading churchmen may have been influenced by a greater degree of exposure to continental design than was the case for secular leadership. Trips to Rome made by English monarchs – even Cnut, the former Viking – exposed these men and their companions to new ideas in dress, architecture and ornamentation.

The doling out of land under the Norman kings to their barons and favourites meant increased activity and development for some locations – the former Anglo-Saxon site of *Dunelm*, for example, which was chosen as a suitably secure location for the bones of St. Cuthbert when Lindisfarne was no longer safe due to Viking raids. The small religious community remained and the site became a place of veneration. The Norman bishop who was awarded the area, William Walchere, appreciated the defensive military capacity of the site and constructed a large cathedral on the top of the hill as well as a keep. William Walchere was initially on good terms with the Anglo-Scandinavian leader, Earl Waltheof, who had submitted to William I in order to retain his position, but by AD 1071 Waltheof had become embroiled in a local rebellion, was carried off to Winchester and eventually beheaded. William Walchere saw an opportunity for advancement and offered to buy the earldom (i.e. the position of earl), thus combining secular and religious power in a single office. The name *Dunelm* was transformed to Duresme in Norman mouths, and is presently called Durham. With so much wealth concentrated in one place, Durham became the economic powerhouse of the region and the city played a major part in stemming the attacks of the Scots. The Earl-Bishop (later Prince-Bishops) of Durham enjoyed unique legal powers in relation to taxation, and could raise their own armies, create markets, and hold their own parliaments. Durham rivalled London and Winchester as a centre of authority.

Anglo-Saxon Towns With Mints at the Time of Norman Invasion

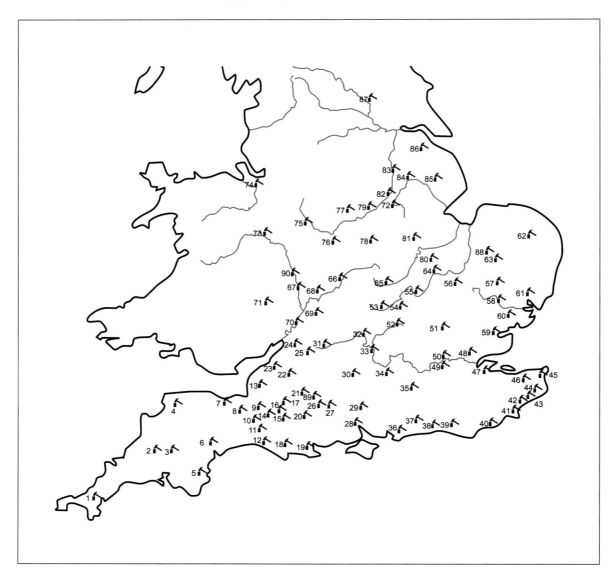

1 Gothabyrig*	24 Berkeley	47 Rochester	70 Gloucester
2 Launceston	25 Malmesbury	48 Horndon	71 Hereford
3 Lydford	26 Wilton	49 Southwark	72 Grantham*
4 Barnstaple	27 Salisbury	50 London	73 Shrewsbury
5 Totnes	28 Southampton	51 Hertford	74 Chester
6 Exeter	29 Winchester	52 Aylesbury	75 Stafford
7 Watchet	30 Bedwyn	53 Buckingham	76 Tamworth
8 Taunton	31 Cricklade	54 Newport Pagnell	77 Derby
9 Langport	32 Oxford	55 Bedford	78 Leicester
10 Petherton	33 Wallingford	56 Cambridge	79 Nottingham
11 Crewkerne	34 Reading	57 Bury St Edmunds	80 Melton Mowes
12 Bridport	35 Guildford	58 Sudbury	81 Stamford
13 Axbridge	36 Chichester	59 Maldon	82 Newark
14 Ilchester	37 Cissbury	60 Colchester	83 Torksey
15 Milborne Port	38 Steyning	61 Ipswich	84 Lincoln
16 Cadbury	39 Lewes	62 Norwich	85 Horncastle
17 Bruton	40 Hastings	63 Thetford	86 Caistor
18 Dorchester	41 Romney	64 Huntingdon	87 York
19 Wareham	42 Lympne	65 Northampton	88 Wilton North
20 Shaftesbury	43 Hythe	66 Warwick	89 Frome
21 Warminster	44 Dover	67 Worcester	90 Droitwich
22 Bath	45 Sandwich	68 Pershore	
23 Bristol	46 Canterbury	69 Winchombe	*Location uncertain

Art Styles

M iddle Saxon art – the Insular and Trewhiddle Styles – drew on the inspiration of the old heathen art of northern Europe, combined with the contemporary Carolingian artistic tradition, based on the Christian idea of representational, message-based iconographic art. The influence of Scandinavian design on Middle Saxon art was negligible, presumably because the two art-styles were being used as badges of identity by political units which were struggling to overcome each other. During the Anglo-Scandinavian Period, aspects of 'Viking' design became more acceptable and Scandinavians in England were able to use elements of their own artistic traditions. The Normans had no specific art style of their own, but used the contemporary Romanesque Style which was already known in Anglo-Saxon England.

Mammen Style

The Scandinavian Mammen Style remained in use from ca. AD 950 to ca. 1025, or possibly a little later in some areas (see *British Artefacts – volume 2: Middle Saxon and Viking*). In Mammen Style, the decoration consists mainly of animals with hatched infill and spiral hips. The Mammen Style was perhaps a transitional stage between the Jelling and the Ringerike Styles. It is named after the decoration on an axe-head found in a grave at Mammen, Denmark.

What to look for: animals with wide bodies and heavy infill, plant tendrils around the body, large spiral hips.

Winchester Style

The Late Saxon Winchester Style was widely used in manuscript art to produce lively, 'busy' illustrations. It draws on both Anglo-Saxon rhythmic decoration and Mediterranean motifs such as the acanthus leaf, and is associated mainly with the scriptoria of the Wessex capital at Winchester but was probably also produced at Canterbury and perhaps elsewhere in southern England in

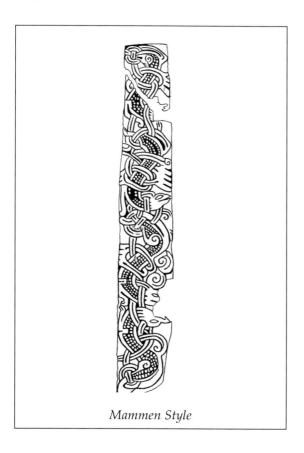

Mammen Style

Winchester Style

the 10th and early 11th centuries. The style was modified when artists at Canterbury were influenced by documents such as the *Utrecht Psalter* with more fluid forms of illustration. In metalwork, the Winchester Style is characterised by use of acanthus-leaf decoration in regular layouts.

What to look for: vegetation with thick fleshy leaves arranged symmetrically.

Ringerike Style

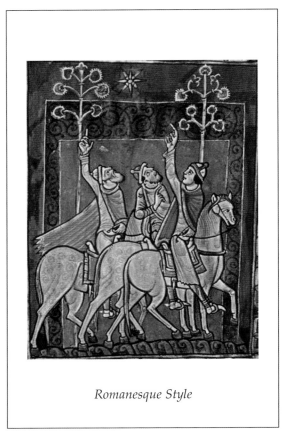

Romanesque Style

Ringerike Style

Ringerike Style is a Scandinavian form of animal-based ornament in use from the late 10th century into the 11th century (circa 980 to circa 1080). It evolved out of the earlier Mammen and Jelling Styles and uses 'lions' (i.e. four-legged animals, often shown walking forwards, with various tendrils protruding from their bodies), birds and serpents. It is named from the ornament on some runestones in Norway, in the Ringerike district north of Oslo. There are some innovations, such as crosses, palmettes and loops binding motifs together. The style probably reflects the reaction of Scandinavian artists using Mammen Style to new influences from both Anglo-Saxon England and the Ottonian Empire.

What to look for: animals with spiral hips, surrounded by a mesh of heavy plant tendrils.

Romanesque Style

Romanesque Style is associated in England primarily with the increased Norman influence from circa AD 1050 but occasional examples of Romanesque art in England may pre-date this by some decades. Romanesque art was used widely across Europe (mainly in France Germany and Italy but also in Spain and as far away as Serbia) from around AD 1000 as an international style of decoration, influenced by Byzantine models. In Romanesque art, the scenes are usually enclosed within a tight frame, and the extremities of the figures often escape from this. The depiction of humans is naturalistic but with some very formal draperies and plant-based ornament. Some details – such as entwined and opposed animals – are probably drawn from Middle Saxon Insular Style but the overall effect of the Romanesque is representational rather than symbolic or geometric. The best-known example of early English Romanesque art is the Bayeux Tapestry, in which the figures are shown in natural poses but the details of the scenery and frames are highly stylised.

What to look for: naturalistic animals and figures, with slender proportions, escaping from tight geometric frames.

Urnes Style

Urnes Style, the last vestige of the Viking artistic tradition, was introduced around AD 1040 and remained in use until ca. 1150 in parts of Scandinavia. It is named after the decoration on the Urnes stave church in Norway, but the majority of objects decorated in Urnes Style are Swedish runestones (whence the alternative name, the Runestone Style). It is characterised by slender, stylised animals interwoven into tight patterns with curled vegetation. The animals are shown in profile, with almond-shaped eyes.

In Scandinavia, the style is divided into early, middle and late phases, which can be quite closely dated. Urnes Style merged with Romanesque style (to form a hybrid Urnes-Romanesque) by around AD 1100 when Christianity became the dominant religious tradition in Scandinavia.

What to look for: animals in profile, with slender proportions and graceful curves, amid tightly curled, narrow tendrils.

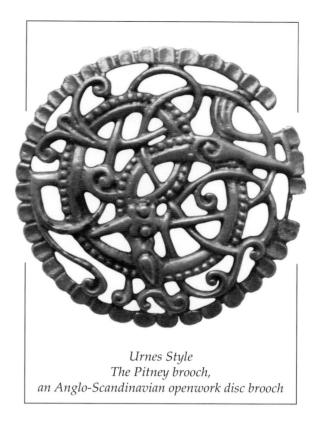

Urnes Style
The Pitney brooch,
an Anglo-Scandinavian openwork disc brooch

Advice for Collectors

Metal and ceramic artefacts from the Anglo-Scandinavian and Norman periods are not as common as Roman coins or clay-pipe stems, and specifically Norman finds, even coins, are rare indeed. They therefore have a monetary value based in part on their rarity, as well as their historical interest and their intrinsic beauty or workmanship.

Some classes of Anglo-Saxon and Viking artefacts are nevertheless quite plentiful (i.e. stirrup mounts) and the interested student can build a respectable collection including examples of the commoner kinds of coin, strap-end and brooch without spending a fortune. Most finds are fragmentary, either having been broken in antiquity and lost by the original owner, or due to many centuries in the plough-soil. Intact examples of the larger types of brooch therefore attract a great deal of attention and can be very valuable. A collector who is prepared to accept damaged, partial or less well-made pieces will find examples of the major types of artefact available for modest sums of money.

It is certainly possible to create the basis of a collection from your own finds, but it is time-consuming, hard work and frustrating. More likely, you will want to supplement your material and complete your collection by buying objects to fill in the gaps. In this case, you should approach a reputable and established antiquities dealer who will be able to offer you advice on the likely cost and availability. You may have objects which you are prepared to sell or exchange, so an element of negotiation will be present.

Before agreeing to buy an object, you should satisfy yourself about the following points:

(i) Does the seller have legal title to the object? Any reputable dealer will be happy to provide a written declaration to this effect.

(ii) Where was the object found? While the dealer may be unable to give you the Ordnance Survey grid reference for the find-spot, he should be able to identify the nearest town or village, and be willing to commit this to writing. The law in Scotland is different from England and Wales, and finds made there have stricter reporting requirements. Some Anglo-Saxon artefacts can be found in Scotland, since the south and south-east was historically part of Bernicia, a division of Anglo-Saxon Northumbria. Viking Age finds are not unknown in both eastern and western Scotland due to the considerable traffic to and from Norway and Ireland which used the Scottish coast for landfall.

(iii) When was the object found? The law concerning Treasure Trove changed in 1997, and this may have a bearing on the legal title issue (see (i)). Dealers often buy whole collections (for example, on the death of the owner, as part of the disposal of his estate) and will be able to advise about this.

(iv) Has the find been reported? Apart from the various legal issues, there is also the consideration that a properly reported find is a 'known quantity' and therefore has greater monetary value. Finds from older collections may not have been formally reported. If the collector did not keep records of his purchases, it may not be possible to establish the provenance for items in the collection; this will affect the market value.

(v) Is the find genuine? While the humbler types of brooch and strap end seldom sell for sums that would make forgery attractive, it is always a possibility. There is also the constant problem of misidentification: some lower-status or fragmentary Anglo-Saxon and Viking finds are similar to Roman and medieval objects. Again, a reputable and experienced dealer should be willing to provide an outline description of the piece, its likely date of manufacture and a written guarantee of authenticity.

While informal transactions may seem attractive to the collector with a limited budget, the risk of fraudulent misrepresentation or simple ignorance on the part of the seller makes it unwise to make such purchases.

Valuations

Throughout this book we offer valuation scales for the various classes of object, which are included for indicative purposes only. Generally we provide two valuations, corresponding to "Fine" and "Very Fine" grades, which relates to the overall condition of the objects as a whole.

The finest pieces of Anglo-Scandinavian metalwork were normally either made from gold or were gilded. This coating preserves the surface of the piece and retains even the finest detailing. Where the gilding has subsequently worn away, the surface is often either pitted and corroded, or worn smooth and featureless. There can therefore be a large difference between the appearance of a gilded object which retains its gilding and that of one which has lost it. This difference in appearance is also reflected in the market price achievable for such objects, with gold or heavily gilded objects usually attracting a substantial premium due to their condition.

We also offer valuations for some of the items illustrated in the listings here. These again are indicative only, and refer in many cases to the specific piece, the value of which may be affected also by its rarity and historical interest. The antiquities market is driven by many factors beyond mere supply and demand, and the valuations shown are correct at the time of going to press but are naturally subject to change.

How to Use the Valuation Scales

The objects and object-types shown in these pages are set out in series, with a decimal classification number (e.g. 1.1 metal brooches, 1.2 metal buckles and so on). A series of current market valuations for each of these types can be found at:

www.british-artefacts.co.uk

The artefacts are classified according to the system employed throughout this book. In order to maintain current, market-related information on the website, the valuations for each class and object will be re-assessed periodically.

Advice for Finders

Finds of Anglo-Scandinavian material are not uncommon in England, although the majority of individual pieces are stirrup mounts and the various types of coin. If you are lucky enough to find Anglo-Scandinavian objects, you should be aware of the legal requirements concerning reporting to the authorities and the best way to conserve and present your finds.

Under the Treasure Act 1996, finders of gold and silver objects, and groups of coins from the same find-spot over 300 years old, have a legal obligation to report them. This provision obviously covers all Anglo-Saxon Viking (including Hiberno-Norse) and Norman material made in precious metal. Changes to the act in late 2009 mean that it is no longer the responsibility of the finder alone – anybody who holds potential treasure in his or her possession must report it within 14 days of becoming aware that it may be covered by the act. It is no longer a defence in law to claim that the finder must have reported the items – it is now an offence to keep such items without knowing that they have been reported. Accurate documentation will be of critical importance in the future.

The body to contact is the local Finds Liaison Officer (FLO) of the Portable Antiquities Scheme (PAS) whom you can find through your local museum, library or the PAS website. Other material is not 'treasure' as defined by the act, and recording is voluntary (in England and Wales; in Scotland, it is compulsory). Finds from the beach or sea are not technically 'treasure' and have to be reported to the 'Receiver of Wreck' which is part of the Coastguard.

Hoards of coins are perhaps a grey area – legally, a hoard is a group of coins from one spot, but in the nature of the case any finds from the plough-soil are likely to be disturbed and redistributed, some damaged and rendered unidentifiable. Therefore if a large number of similar-period coins appear in a restricted area, it is wisest to assume that they once formed a hoard and are not simply a random accumulation of dropped money. The value of a hoard is greater than that of the individual coins – both in terms of historical interest and financially. A few casually dropped coins do not provide much information, but a collection of coins gathered together and buried implies both a level of portable wealth for somebody in the area and also a level of perceived threat.

Reporting your finds is useful, since the FLO will help you to identify them and may be able to suggest further research to help you understand the subject in more detail. In isolation, a single find may mean very little but as part of the larger picture, local or regional, it can show where settlements and markets were situated, which will allow the local archaeologists to make sure that proper investigations are made when building work and other soil disturbance is scheduled to take place in that area. Your find may be of an unusual type, or one not normally associated with your area: in such cases, it will have a statistical importance to the history of the subject – both the typology of the object-class and potentially the history of your area - beyond what is immediately apparent. Until the object is reported, it will be very difficult to find this out.

Conservation is a difficult business, and it is all too easy to destroy the value of an item by overzealous cleaning. Loose soil should be removed to determine what the object is, but any pieces which are more firmly attached should be left in place. Your museum or FLO will be able to advise you on the appropriate method, and if you are intending to sell it or have it valued by a dealer he may be prepared to take this task on for you. You may have to pay a nominal sum for this service, but since the alternative is to risk damage or destruction of the item it is normally worthwhile.

1. Metal Artefacts

The commonest artefact type from the Anglo-Scandinavian and Norman period is the coinage, which runs from the Middle Saxon types in an unbroken sequence to modern times. Late Anglo-Saxon coinage was produced in large quantities for reasons connected in part to burgeoning economic activity, as well as inventive royal taxation and the demands of the *Danegeld*. Coinage produced during the Norman period has often been struck by moneyers with Anglo-Saxon or Anglo-Scandinavian names such as Æþelmer, Godric, Sæwulf. In the reign of King Stephen, there appears to be an increase of Norman-style moneyer names such as Simon.

1.1 BROOCHES

The great variety of plate and bow brooches found in the earlier Anglo-Saxon periods appears to have dwindled to just a few recognised forms by the 11th century. The Bayeux tapestry shows males with their cloaks pinned at the right shoulder by a flat disc with a central roundel – perhaps intended for the enamel cloisonné brooches shown below (section 1.1.1). Anglo-Scandinavian females probably continued to use tortoise brooches with Scandinavian-style costume in areas such as the Kingdom of York which were not content to be homogenised into Late Saxon forms of dress.

The cloak-fastening shown on the famous image of King Cnut (see page 15) appears to be a pair of elaborate strings or laces tied at the shoulder. If this style of organic closure became popular in the 11th century, it would explain why so few metal brooches are found compared to the previous periods.

1.1.1 Disc brooches

Anglo-Scandinavian disc brooches enjoyed a revival in the later 10th or 11th century with the development of a cupped face-plate made in copper-alloy, within which a series of cloisons were created to be filled with brightly coloured enamel. Enamelwork had not previously formed part of the Anglo-Saxon artist's repertoire, other than its occasional use on a few bow brooches in East Anglia. Champ-levé enamelling was a technique adopted by the Anglo-Saxons, perhaps at the end of the 10th century.

Fig.1.1.1-a
(Scale 1.5:1)

Fig.1.1.1-a. A 9th-10th century cast lead disc brooch with cruciform design surrounding a central boss, billetted border to the outer edge; solder scars from lugs and catchplate on the reverse. From a German collection.

Fig.1.1.1-b
(Scale 1:2)

Fig.1.1.1-d
(Scale 1.25:1)

Fig.1.1.1-b. An Anglo-Saxon silver epigraphic disc brooch from Cuxton (Kent), based on the style of legend used on coins. The central motif is a dragon being attacked by an eagle (symbolic of the struggle between good and evil) and the legend reads +ÆLFGIVVMEAH i.e. *Ælfgifu me ah* '(Lady) Ælfgifu own me'.

Fig.1.1.1-d. A sheet bronze discoid repoussé mount with central motif of a regardant beast, cross and pellets surrounded by a band of pseudo-text '+ACA[.]H.+F+F:. MEON' within a pelletted border. It seems likely that the mount was influenced by contemporary coinage. It was found in Norwich, Norfolk and dates from the 9th-11th century AD.

Fig.1.1.1-c
(Scale 2:1)

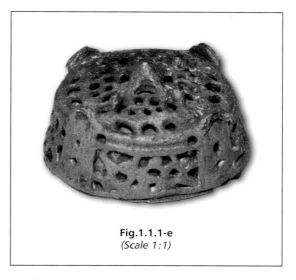

Fig.1.1.1-e
(Scale 1:1)

Fig.1.1.1-c. A silver penny of the reign of Edward the Confessor made into a brooch with the 'reverse' of the coin gilded as the face of the brooch; a copper-alloy pin fitting has been rivetted to the back. The original coin is an Expanding Cross type penny, with the reverse reading +EADREDONLVNDEN: for the moneyer Eadwerd at London mint. It dates from the period AD 1050-1060.

Fig.1.1.1-e. An 11th century AD late Viking type of decorative item is the 'box brooch' in cast bronze formed as an openwork outer shell, an inner container and bottom plate. The upper face has a central conical boss and four small satellite bosses each with a silver surface disc; to the outer face there are four pierced tongue-shaped panels with D-shaped finials proud of the upper face, each with a silvered element to the upper end. The bottom plate features an integral catchplate and central void, with four attachment pins to the underside; the upper face and sidewall are executed in Urnes Style zoomorphic openwork. The inner element is a sheet bronze container. From a private collection.

Fig.1.1.1-f
(Scale 1.25:1)

Fig.1.1.1-f. Although a 10th century fashion, Borre style brooches probably continued in use in England into the 11th century. This is a bronze disc brooch, slightly domed, with Borre style interlace design to the face, pin-lugs and catchplate to the reverse. It was found at Seighford, Staffordshire.

Fig.1.1.1-g
(Scale 1.25:1)

Fig.1.1.1-g. A 10th-11th century AD gilt-bronze disc brooch, again slightly domed, with Borre style interlace design to the face, pin-lugs, catchplate and attachment loop to the reverse. It was found at Dragonby, Lincolnshire.

Fig.1.1.1-h
(Scale 1.5:1)

Fig.1.1.1-h. An 11th century cast gilt-bronze disc brooch with cruciform cells and seven lobes surrounding, containing blue enamel infill; pin, pin-lugs and catchplate complete on the reverse. It was found in East Anglia.

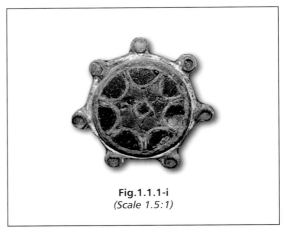

Fig.1.1.1-i
(Scale 1.5:1)

Fig.1.1.1-i. An unusual cloisonné brooch with a radiating 'hub-and-spokes' design in green, dark blue and pale blue enamel. Around the circumference are the standard seven lobed projections, three of them still with their inlays of blue and translucent 'jewels'. It was found in Lancashire.

Fig.1.1.1-j
(Scale 1.5:1)

Fig.1.1.1-j. A beautiful gilt copper-alloy brooch with enamel cloisonné decoration in blue, red, green and white. The design is a standard La Tène pattern of a central triangle whose apices extend to form the borders of three fields, each with a double volute end. Germanic (Anglo-Saxon, Frankish and Scandinavian) craftsmen made almost no use of enamelling as a decorative technique; in the 7th century AD the art was introduced by contact with Byzantine craftsmen. Among the Romano-Britons and Irish, enamelling had remained a standard form of metallic surface decoration. The 10th century efflorescence of enamel decoration stems from changing tastes, perhaps connected to religious reform but more probably due to the increasing difficulty in obtaining other materials (e.g. millefiori glass) which had been the preferred Germanic media for several centuries. This example lacks the satellite bosses which are a standard feature of the type. The brooch was found in Cambridgeshire.

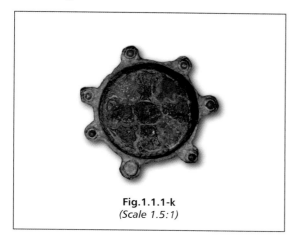

Fig.1.1.1-k
(Scale 1.5:1)

Fig.1.1.1-k. An Anglo-Scandinavian enamelled disc brooch of 11th century date, comprising a central enamel disc within a copper-alloy collet, surrounded by seven satellite lobes each with a domed cabochon insert. The enamel panel is constructed as a dark blue saltire with corrugated edges against quadrants of navy blue and turquoise. The brooch was found in Wiltshire.

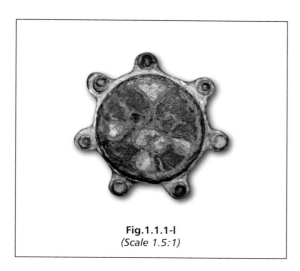

Fig.1.1.1-l
(Scale 1.5:1)

Fig.1.1.1-l. A good example of an Anglo-Scandinavian gilt copper-alloy disc brooch with cloisonné enamel in dark blue, white and yellow. The rim is complete and even retains the seven lobed extensions which are often lost from such brooches. Five of them still have the cabochons still present. This distinctive type of brooch was produced in England during the late 10th and 11th centuries. The brooch was found on the Cambridgeshire/Suffolk border.

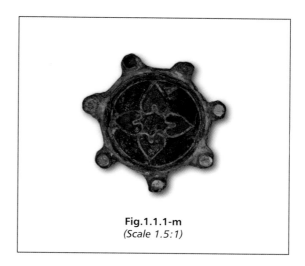

Fig.1.1.1-m
(Scale 1.5:1)

Fig.1.1.1-m. An Anglo-Scandinavian enamelled disc brooch with a 'floral geometric' design consisting of a circular deep-blue background with heart-shaped inserts in blue and green around a central disc with short radiating arms. The enamelwork is contained within a copper-alloy rim which extends to an outer border, from which emerge seven satellite discoid lobes with spherical blue glass inserts of which one remains. The spring lug is in place on the reverse, which is gilded, and the attachment point for the catchplate. The decoration is similar to that on the Brasenose Disc (now in the Ashmolean Museum, Oxford). It was found in County Durham.

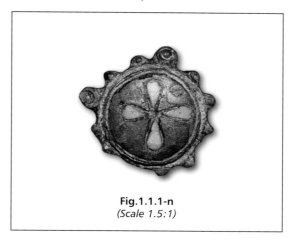

Fig.1.1.1-n
(Scale 1.5:1)

Fig.1.1.1-n. A classic form of Anglo-Scandinavian disc brooch comprising a central enamel panel surrounded by radiating knops filled with enamel cabochons; the junctions for twelve or thirteen knops can be seen around the perimeter. The central panel is a dark blue enamel background with an inset cross formed from four elongated lobes in pale blue enamel. The cruciform design may have been chosen for its religious significance in the mixed Anglo-Saxon and Scandinavian culture of the later 10th and 11th centuries. It was found in Lincolnshire.

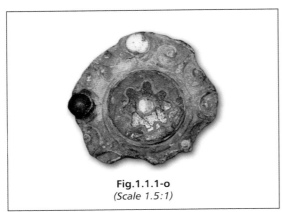

Fig.1.1.1-o
(Scale 1.5:1)

Fig.1.1.1-o. A developed form of disc brooch in which the outer bosses are no longer placed on radiating spikes, but form an outer ring with scrollwork between them. The central design is of the standard hub-and-spokes form, with the spokes terminating short of the outer ring. It was found in Cambridgeshire.

Fig.1.1.1-p
(Scale 1.5:1)

Fig.1.1.1-p. A cloisonné disc brooch with a raised central tray enclosing a floral pattern of four longer and four shorter elliptical leaves, filled with turquoise enamel against a field of dark blue. Around the edge is set a series of six lobes with dark blue cabochons. It was found in Suffolk.

Fig.1.1.1-q
(Scale 1.5:1)

Fig.1.1.1-q. An Anglo-Scandinavian disc brooch comprising a central enamel disc surrounded by seven radiating knops filled with cabochons (three remaining). The central panel is a dark blue enamel background with an inset radiating cloison design in black and turquoise enamel. It was found in East Anglia.

Fig.1.1.1-r
(Scale 1:1)

Fig.1.1.1-r. An 11th century disc brooch from Bedlington, Northumberland, featuring a central champ-levé panel depicting a bird. It was found in a burial mound along with a bone comb, and probably represents the grave one of the last Scandinavians to practise this rite.

Fig.1.1.1-s
(Scale 1.5:1)

Fig.1.1.1-s. A very rare William I nummular brooch probably made around AD 1070. Nummular brooches with designs based on contemporary coin types were used as small clothing fasteners. The design shows a facing bust below a 'canopy' (also found on other coins of this monarch) with the legend +BENNOMEVECIT 'Benno made me' around the rim. It was found in Cambridgeshire.

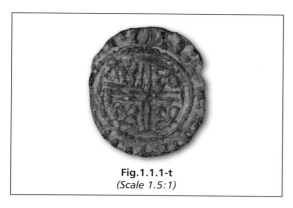

Fig.1.1.1-t
(Scale 1.5:1)

Fig.1.1.1-t. This nummular brooch has a central motif of a voided cross with fleurs-de-lys in the quarters, surrounded by a pelletted band. In the outer field is the legend, now fragmentary. The reverse bears signs of the manufacture by the repoussé method; attachment points for the hinge and catchplate are visible. The coin-type is a recognised issue of Henry I (AD 1100-35) whose early reign coincided with a period of monetary crisis in which there was great public scepticism about the quality of the coinage; Henry's purge of moneyers in England in AD 1124 did much to rectify the problem and restore confidence. It was found in Hampshire.

1.1.2 Plate Brooches

The Viking styles of brooch remained in production in Anglo-Saxon England into the 11th century, but were gradually replaced.

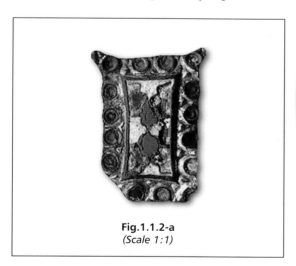

Fig.1.1.2-a
(Scale 1:1)

Fig.1.1.2-a. An unusual quadrangular plate brooch cast in copper-alloy and gilded, with enamel champ-levé decoration in the centre and enamel-filled cells around the edges. The rectangular form is unusual for this period, but the technique and the surrounding lobes are similar to the Anglo-Scandinavian disc brooches in section 1.1.1. It was found in north-east Lincolnshire.

Fig.1.1.2-b
(Scale 1:1)

Fig.1.1.2-b. A lozengiform plate brooch with radiating floral decoration, heavily gilded. At the centre and at the middle of each of the sides is placed a large silver domed rivet, forming a quincunx pattern. The pin and pin-lug are in place on the reverse; the attachment point for the missing catchplate can be discerned. The decoration of the brooch is typical of the Late Anglo-Saxon Winchester Style, seen in manuscripts such as the *Ramsey Psalter*. Prominent domed rivets are found on contemporary high-status objects such as the Sutton (Isle of Ely) brooch. It was found in Suffolk.

Fig.1.1.2-c
(Scale 1:1)

Fig.1.1.2-c. A pair of 10th-11th century cast bronze tortoise brooches each comprising an elliptical boss with flat surround; the boss with four lugs and relief decoration, the surround pierced at the top for attachment of a chain; to the reverse pin-lugs and catchplate are in place; one brooch with an ancient repair to a lug. Tortoise brooches were worn high on the chest with a swag of glass and amber beads between.

Fig.1.1.2-d
(Scale 1:1)

Fig.1.1.2-d. A 10th century cast bronze elliptical tortoise brooch with a broad rim and domed centre bearing Mammen Style decoration including a pair of opposed birds' heads. The Scandinavian artistic tradition remained firmly rooted in the imagery of the Viking past, even when the users were already beginning to convert to Christianity. It was found in Alnwick.

1.1.3 Zoomorphic Brooches

Zoomorphic brooches were a long-lived tradition in Anglo-Saxon and Scandinavian communities. Most types appear to have fallen into disuse in the 11th century, but the overtly Christian bird-and-cross type continued.

Fig.1.1.3-a
(Scale 1.5:1)

Fig.1.1.3-a. A rare type of Middle Saxon openwork bird brooch (see *British Artefacts vol. 2*) still used in Anglo-Scandinavian England, it comprises a bird facing right with large fanned tail decorated with incised lines to represent the plumage. The head has a large lentoid eye; the body bears a piriform wing behind which the cross is tucked. The feet and lower end of the cross are carefully modelled: this feature is usually missing from brooches of this kind, perhaps because the thin projection was liable to damage. It was found in Cambridgeshire.

Fig.1.1.3-b
(Scale 1.5:1)

Fig.1.1.3-b. A rare type of the standard Anglo-Scandinavian plate brooch formed as a stylised bird with a cross on its back. The bird's body shows a pear-shaped wing, a transverse-ribbed collar on the lower body from which a trapezoidal tail emerges, decorated with flaring lines to show the feathers. The bird's eye and beak are modelled, and there is an internal border to the cross. Most unusually, the present brooch has retained the lower end of the cross by the bird's feet, and a portion of the branch on which the bird is perching. The significance of the brooch lies in the religious symbolism of the dove of Christ bearing the cross. It was found at North Wickford, Essex and dates from the 10th century AD.

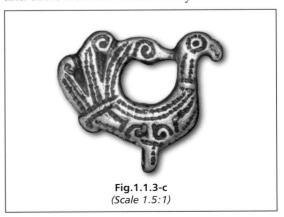

Fig.1.1.3-c
(Scale 1.5:1)

Fig.1.1.3-c. A cast silver brooch in the form of a stylised bird with punched-point lines to the tail, body and neck, and scrolls to the body and tail. There are transverse bands at the neck and rump and, below, a pierced lug for the attachment of a chain. To the reverse, there are solder scars indicating where the pin-lug and catchplate were attached, but the pin was lost in antiquity. It is a Viking artefact of 10th-11th century date.

Fig.1.1.3-e
(Scale 1.5:1)

Fig.1.1.3-d
(Scale 1.5:1)

Fig.1.1.3-d. A cast bronze brooch in the form of a bird standing on a branch with projecting wing and comb. It is a Viking type of 9th-10th century date.

Fig.1.1.3-e. An important type of zoomorphic brooch is the 'Valkyrie and Horseman' class of 9th-10th century date. Above is a cast bronze plate brooch with an openwork design depicting a horseman facing right with a spear in his right hand facing a standing robed female figure bearing a shield. The pin lug and catchplate are in place on the reverse. The scene probably represents the arrival of a fallen warrior at Valhalla where he is greeted by an armed valkyrie. This imagery was popular in the Viking period and is used in the poem *Eiriksmál* commemorating the death of King Erik Bloodaxe on Stainmoor, Yorkshire in AD 954. It was found in Nottingham.

Fig.1.1.3-f
(Scale 1.5:1)

Fig.1.1.3-f A cast bronze trefoil brooch with three arms issuing from a central triangle. At the junctions of the arms and centre are grotesque faces in high relief and regular scrolled ornament within a pelletted border. The brooch is in a private collection.

Fig.1.1.3-g
(Scale 1:1)

Fig.1.1.3-g A cast bronze trefoil brooch, less detailed than the previous example, and with flatter decoration. The grotesque faces are placed at the outer ends of the arms which are filled with three-band knotwork. It is in a private collection.

1.1.4 Penannular Brooches

Penannular brooches became popular in Anglo-Scandinavian society, probably due to influence from the Hiberno-Norse who used large examples with dangerously long pins as a badge of wealth and status.

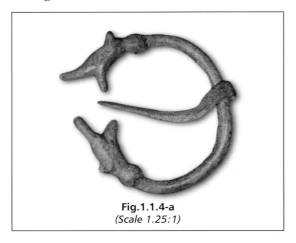

Fig.1.1.4-a
(Scale 1.25:1)

Fig.1.1.4-a. An unusual form of penannular brooch with zoomorphic terminals. The band is formed as a round-section bar ending in bulbous collars and naturalistic lupine heads with gaping mouths and protrusive ears. Penannular brooches date back to the Bronze Age, and most have simple clubbed or scrolled terminals; examples with animal-head terminals are often associated with the Baltic

Vikings where they may have had religious significance. In Norse tradition, a pair of wolves, Skoll and Hatti, chased the sun and moon across the sky and would eventually catch them at the end of the world. The design of the heads on this brooch is similar to the Urnes Style decoration with lentoid eyes. It was found in Hampshire.

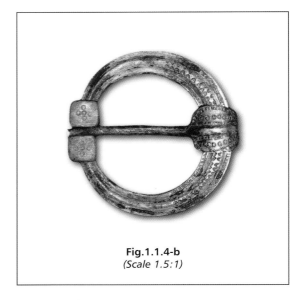

Fig.1.1.4-b
(Scale 1.5:1)

Fig.1.1.4-b. A silver penannular brooch with rectangular terminals with a punched quincunx decoration, typical of Baltic Viking techniques which continued in use into the Middle Ages in the eastern Baltic (e.g. Selonia, Semigalia). The band is a flat casting with a central raised ridge, the outer semicircle detailed with punched pellet ornamentation. The pin is a round-section rod expanding to lateral flanges where it loops around the band, bearing similar punched decoration. It is of Baltic origin.

1.1.5 Annular Brooches

Annular brooches are not a common type in the 11th century but occasional examples are found.

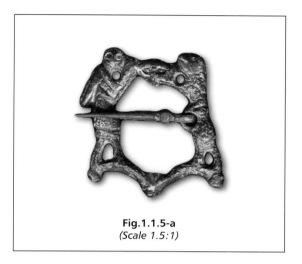

Fig.1.1.5-a
(Scale 1.5:1)

Fig.1.1.5-a. A gilt medieval brooch showing an angel to the left facing right, wrestling with a lion facing left, between them is a human head, clamped between the tussling arms of the lion and angel. There are very few recorded examples of this English brooch type, and we can find no record of one with a human head between an angel and lion. Findspot unknown, dates from the 12th or 13th century AD.

1.2 BUCKLES & BELT FITTINGS

Belt buckles retreated from the exuberance of the earlier Middle Saxon period and became rather understated and functional. Romanesque ornament on the plate identifies Norman equipment, and the taste for buckle-loops with faces is a curiosity of the 12th century.

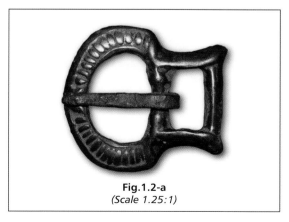

Fig.1.2-a
(Scale 1.25:1)

Fig.1.2–a. A decorative buckle of Scandinavian Baltic type. The broad loop is ornamented with transverse billeted detailing within a frame. The lower edge of the loop meets the tongue-bar and extends to form an integral quadrangular keeper with flared lateral edges. The central outer portion of the loop forms a couch for the scrolled iron tongue. It was found in Lincolnshire.

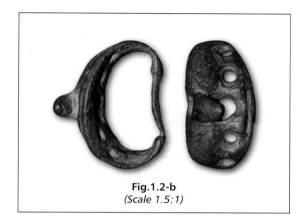

Fig.1.2-b
(Scale 1.5:1)

Fig.1.2-b. An openwork buckle loop modelled in the round. The bar for the tongue is very fine (about 1.5 mm) expanding into an elliptical cast loop with five circular recesses in the lower edge. The upper edge comprises a protruding bird-head feature flanked by curved wings extending back to the bar; behind the bird's head is a small circular couch for the end of the tongue. The loop is of hollowed D-section with a pronounced carination. The raven was a significant animal in Norse culture, with a role in several myths connected with the *Óðinn* cult; it appears on warriors' equipment from as early as the Vendel culture of the 6th century with cognates in the Baltic region and Anglo-Saxon England (i.e. the Sutton Hoo shield). It was found in Suffolk.

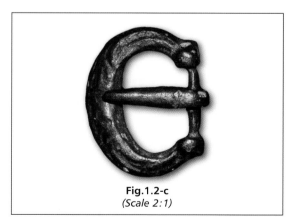

Fig.1.2-c
(Scale 2:1)

Fig.1.2-c. An Anglo-Scandinavian buckle formed as a dished D-shaped loop with thickened disc terminals and a thin rear bar. The tongue is a broad, flat triangle looped around the bar. The outer edge of the loop is decorated with cast linear ornament in a Scandinavian-influenced Winchester Style. It was found in Yorkshire.

Fig.1.2-d
(Scale 1.5:1)

Fig.1.2-d. A late Viking or Anglo-Scandinavian cast openwork buckle in Urnes Style of the 11th century AD. The D-shaped buckle has a bulb at the lower point in the form of a human head with bulbous brow and nose, and with arms raised; above this the plate is constructed as a tracery of tendrils extending to both ends of the rear bar which is gripped in the jaws of two beasts. The motif of the man with his arms raised to his head, gripping his hair, is of some antiquity and is found on Merovingian period decorative metalwork of the 5th-7th century; it appears to be connected to the notion of the hair as a continuously renewing resource, and thus an emblem of eternal rebirth. In Scandinavia, such ideas were associated with the group of gods called the *Vanir* among whom *Freyr* and *Njorðr* are the principal males. It was found in Sleaford, Lincolnshire.

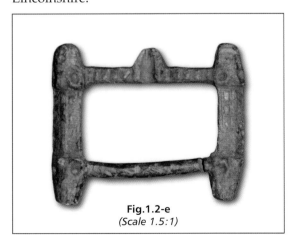

Fig.1.2-e
(Scale 1.5:1)

Fig.1.2-e. An unusual rectangular belt buckle of Scandinavian type. The forward bar is segmented with a triangular couch for the tongue (lost in antiquity); the side bars are chamfered, with segment detailing on both

outer surfaces; the rear bar is round in section. At each corner is placed a triangular beast-head motif with square muzzle and two prominent, rounded ears, those on the forward edge facing forwards and those on the rear facing backwards. Buckles with similar decoration in triangular form are known from Viking period sites, but the rectangular style is very rare. It was found near Kemble, Gloucestershire.

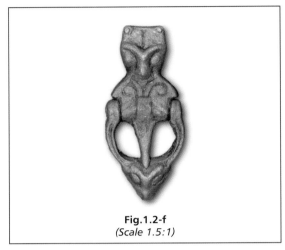

Fig.1.2-f
(Scale 1.5:1)

Fig.1.2-f. A 10th-11th century hinged, two-piece buckle, comprising a triangular beast-head with prominent brow and eyes above a D-shaped panel bearing Ringerike Style scrolled patterning developing into an integral pointed, triangular tongue. The D-shaped loop thickens on the outer edge to a second beast-head. The upper section is split longitudinally to accept the strap, with two small rivets still in situ.

Fig.1.2-g
(Scale 1.25:1)

Fig.1.2-g. An Anglo-Norman copper-alloy belt buckle with a Romanesque Style griffin executed in enamel champ-levé on the plate. The loop is kidney-shaped with a thickened couch for the tongue. The plate is folded to trap the leather belt between the two faces, secured with two rivets. It was found in North Essex.

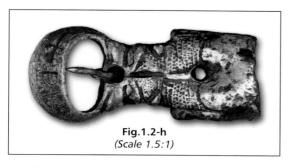

Fig.1.2-h.
(Scale 1.5:1)

Fig.1.2-h. An 11th-12th century AD cast bronze buckle with silvered surface formed as a rectangular plate and animal-head developing into a broad loop; the tongue is a pointed wire looped through a hole in the plate; on the outer surface of the loop is the text '+PR' with decorative elements before and after; a zone of punched decoration is above the animal head and the plate is curved with a single rivet-hole. It was found in Cambridgeshire in the early 1990s.

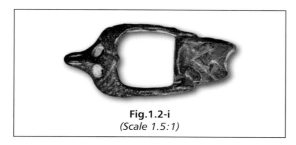

Fig.1.2-i
(Scale 1.5:1)

Fig.1.2-i. A narrow, copper-alloy buckle comprising a fine copper-alloy strap with surface tooling, looped over the rear bar of the buckle; the leading edge is in the form of a sharply-beaked bird-head, the eyes indicated by circular holes and feathers by ridged decoration around the sides. There is no tongue: the strap was held by a spike emerging from the back of the face. This form of buckle may date from the later 11th or 12th century, and have been introduced by the Normans. It was found in Cambridgeshire.

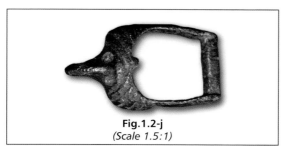

Fig.1.2-j
(Scale 1.5:1)

Fig.1.2-j. A copper-alloy buckle with its leading edge in the form of a bird-head with a prominent hooked beak. The narrow aperture and lack of a separate tongue make it likely that these buckles were used on straps which needed to be released quickly. It was found in Cambridgeshire.

Fig.1.2-k
(Scale 1.5:1)

Fig.1.2-k. A narrow buckle with its leading edge in the form of a beast with a prominent muzzle, the eyes indicated by circular holes and the mane by ridged decoration across the back. There is no tongue. It was found at Snettisham, Norfolk, and it dates from the 11th-12th century AD.

Fig.1.2-l
(Scale 1.5:1)

Fig.1.2-l. A Romanesque style buckle plate with two large attachment rivets. The design is an advancing lion facing outwards, with a raised tail and one raised forepaw; it pre-figures the formal heraldic lion of the later medieval period in its 'passant gardant' pose. From the Kennis collection.

Fig.1.2-m
(Scale 1.5:1)

Fig.1.2-m. A cast copper-alloy buckle formed with a broad elliptical loop, decorated with undulating lines of punched-point detailing and pierced in four places. Opposite the tongue is an integrally cast human mask with triangular eyes, slit mouth, prominent ears and nose. The tongue is a flat-section bar looped around the rear edge of the loop, with a simple collar to the rear. It was found in Marlborough, Wiltshire.

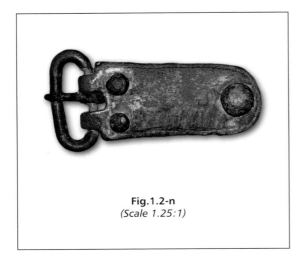

Fig.1.2-n
(Scale 1.25:1)

Fig.1.2-o
(Scale 1.5:1)

Fig.1.2-n. A complete example of an early medieval 12th century AD strap end buckle, with plate bow and pin all preserved. The plate has a simple border line decoration with traces of gilding and three rivets; two for attaching the bow and the third to affix the buckle to a leather strap. The simple bow and pin are fully functional. It was found in Hertfordshire.

Fig.1.2-o. A 10th-11th century beautifully-made late Anglo-Saxon buckle loop, slightly dished in profile, showing Scandinavian influence in the execution of the zoomorphs. The round-section bar is held between two drooping animal-heads with bulbous, ovoid eyes and c-scroll ears. A ribbed central collar forms the rest for the tongue. It was found in Cambridgeshire.

Fig.1.2-p
(Scale 2:1)

Fig.1.2-p. A 12th-13th century cast copper-alloy belt mount with gilding to the surface and reserved design. To each end is a column of four rivet holes (four still present) and to the centre a column of three (all present). The central column bisects a design of two lions rampant with hatched necks reserved against a champ-levé field with traces of red enamel. It was acquired in London in 1990.

42

Fig.1.2-q
(Scale 2:1)

Fig.1.2-q. A 12th-13th century cast copper-alloy belt mount with gilding to the surface and reserved design. To each end are four holes for attachment rivets, one in situ to each end, on a vertical border. The central motif is a reserved sea lion regardant with forelegs supporting the body, the tail and fins extended to the rear; remains of the red enamel are present in the field close to the jaw and neck. The upper body and tail are hatched, the lower body panelled. It was acquired in London in 1988.

1.3 STRAP ENDS

Strap ends and decorative tags continued to form part of the suite of belt fittings, and examples are found in all the main decorative styles of the period. Strap ends with Winchester Style decoration are a fairly common find in some parts of England.

Fig.1.3-a. A thick, cast strap end in silver-gilt, with decorative elements in high relief. The design comprises a cross with central boss, between the arms of which are four similar bosses within semicircles. A raised bar runs across the top beyond which is the thinner bar pierced for attachment. Similar D-shaped strap ends are a Late Saxon development influenced by contemporary Scandinavian fashions; the heavy moulding and geometric design are based on Winchester Style manuscript decoration and its derivatives in the plastic arts. It originates from the Netherlands.

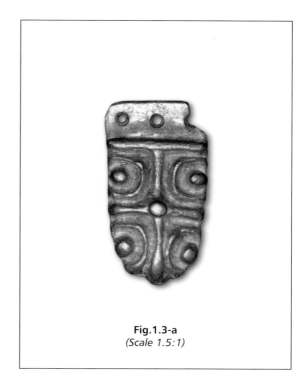

Fig.1.3-a
(Scale 1.5:1)

Fig.1.3-b
(Scale 1.5:1)

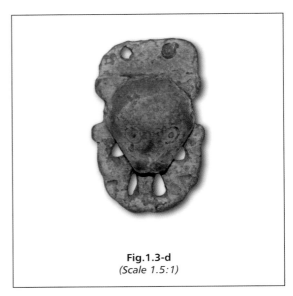

Fig.1.3-d
(Scale 1.5:1)

Fig.1.3-b. Late Saxon 'Class E' strap ends are tongue-shaped and often decorated with plant-based ornament in the Winchester Style. The present example is of the classic profile, but has a bilinear knotwork panel within a ring-and-dot border. The casting features a split in the upper edge to accommodate the leather strap or belt to which it was attached. Similar forms were used by Anglo-Scandinavians and Vikings in the British Isles. It was found in East Anglia.

Fig.1.3-d. A cast copper-alloy strap end of Thomas's Class E type 1 variant, tongue-shaped with a straight attachment end and rounded terminal. The attachment end features two circular rivet holes, one filled with corrosion. Below, it features a bear's head modelled in the round with semi circular ears, slight brow ridges and short blunt muzzle. Inlaid niello ring-and-dot forms the eyes. From the mouth project branching tendrils forming the rounded terminal executed in openwork. It was found at Cossington, Somerset.

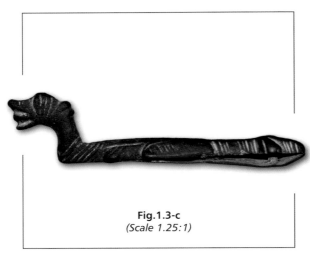

Fig.1.3-c
(Scale 1.25:1)

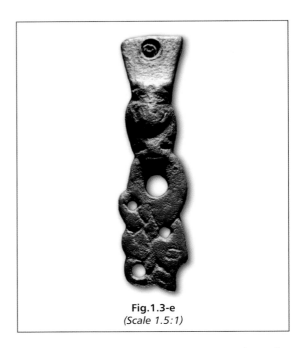

Fig.1.3-e
(Scale 1.5:1)

Fig.1.3-c. An unusual zoomorphic strap end modelled in the round. The upper terminal displays a three-lobed design with ribbed detailing along the sides. This extends along the length of the main body which features folded wings and lobed shoulders. At the lower end, a skilfully modelled neck develops at right-angles to the body, arching gracefully down to a robust animal-head finial with open mouth and extended tongue. Aspects of the detailing recall Ringerike style, such as the semi-naturalistic treatment of the animal's head and wings. It was found in Norfolk.

Fig.1.3-e. A remarkable strap end in the form of a knotwork animal executed in openwork in the mouth of a ferocious beast. The style owes much to contemporary Scandinavian taste. The tapering plate is pierced to accept an attachment rivet. From the Kennis collection.

Fig.1.3-f
(Scale 1.5:1)

Fig.1.3-f. A Viking D-shaped strap end cast in copper-alloy with a split upper end. The design comprises as transverse band of pellet-in-square above a stylised male face with a prominent nose and mouth. The left eye is shown round, open and staring while the right is elliptical and closed. In the context of later Viking design, this design can only represent the god *Óðinn* (Odin) who exchanged one of his eyes for a drink of the numinous Mead of Inspiration. The eye was placed in the well of Mimir, and was afterwards known by the poetic name *veð valföðrs* 'the pledge of the father of the slain'. The upper edge of the strap end is pierced in two places for attachment to the belt or harness; the rivets are still in situ. It was found in East Anglia.

Fig.1.3-g
(Scale 1.5:1)

Fig.1.3-g. A late 10th-11th century cast silver strap end with decorative panel bearing Winchester Style foliate decoration, the thick (6 mm) surface gilded; the attachment plate pierced with five holes, with a pronounced (3.5 mm) step to accommodate a substantial belt or strap. Winchester Style is the last native Anglo-Saxon art style to be developed in England before the European Romanesque style became common in the later 11th century. It was found at Salisbury, Wiltshire, England in 1978.

Fig.1.3-h
(Scale 1.25:1)

Fig.1.3-h. An 11th century cast bronze bifacial strap end with Winchester Style foliate ornament and animal mask; above, a rectangular attachment plate pierced in three places. From a private collection, found at Birchinton, Kent.

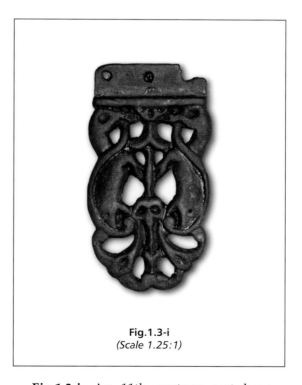

Fig.1.3-i
(Scale 1.25:1)

Fig.1.3-i. An 11th century cast bronze openwork strap end with two rampant beasts biting at a central tree. The design is influenced by Late Saxon Winchester Style but retains the Viking zoomorphic elements. It was found in Wiltshire.

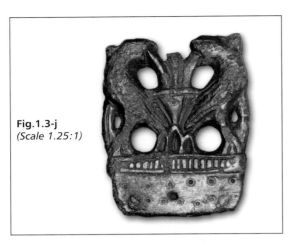

Fig.1.3-j
(Scale 1.25:1)

Fig.1.3-l
(Scale 1.5:1)

Fig.1.3-j. A substantial Viking period strap end cast in copper-alloy openwork. The main motif is a pair of addorsed ravens emerging from the base line, with a central column between them. From their beaks issue tendrils which merge with the central column; the column develops into a funnel-shaped feature with ring-and-dot motif. Along the base is a billeted border above a plain panel with incised ring-and-dot motifs. The top of the central column was lost in antiquity. It is possible that the addorsed ravens represent Huginn and Muninn, the bird-companions of *Óðinn* (Odin) and the funnel is the vessel *Gjallarhorn* which is associated with the eschatological events described in the Old Icelandic poem *Völuspá*. The piece is cast bifacially, with good rounded moulding. It was found near Norwich, Norfolk.

Fig.1.3-l. A cast openwork 12th century tongue-shaped strap end decorated in the Romanesque Style with a long-necked bird amid foliage. The upper bar is pierced to accept two attachment pins and a securing plate, all still in place. It was found at Hastings, Sussex.

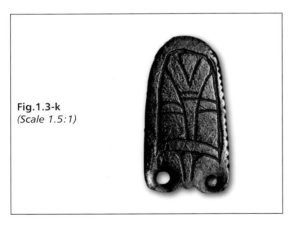

Fig.1.3-k
(Scale 1.5:1)

Fig.1.3-m
(Scale 1.5:1)

Fig.1.3-k. A D-shaped copper-alloy strap end formed with a transverse split through the upper third of its length. The edge is carefully notched to give a beaded effect. The upper edge has two lobed extensions to accommodate the piercings for the attachment rivets, similar to the shape of 9th-10th century Anglo-Saxon strap ends. The internal panel is heater-shaped with an incised Y-shaped design executed in a crude version of Ringerike Style. It was found in East Anglia.

Fig.1.3-m. A rare 11th century Norman zoomorphic strap end, with a rectangular fixing plate ornamented with plain central chevron in double-outline. The terminal converges to a narrow neck, then expands to an everted volute with incised linear decoration. The finial is in the form of the profile head of a 'talbot' or hunting-dog. The eye is prominently marked, with a surrounding border which extends to the entire profile of the dog. The two attachment rivets are still present. It was found in Suffolk.

Fig.1.3-n. A matching suite of three Anglo-Norman openwork copper-alloy belt fittings dating from the later 11th century, all found at Skirpenbeck in Yorkshire.

(a) A cast ball-ended strap end with slightly expanding profile. The outer zone features two circular piercings, terminating in three globular projections. Behind this, the field bears a T-shaped piercing and a double ridged border. The rear edge of the piece features a stepped recess, probably the remains of a cruciform piercing at the point of fracture. Two attachment rivets are in place on the reverse.

(b) A cast strap end similar to the preceding, but with a stepped feature separating two zones. The outer zone comprises a raised panel with two circular piercings, terminating in three globular projections. Behind this, the field is surrounded by an incised border with a T-shaped piercing. The rear edge of the piece features two semi-circular projections from the underside. An attachment rivet is in place on the reverse.

(c) A cast ball-ended strap end with a projecting knop and a raised rib on the inner edge. Two further ribs divide the field into panels: the first features three circular piercings in a triangle formation, the next a lozengiform piercing with finial extensions forming a cruciform pattern; the third a pair of circular piercings on a raised platform. An attachment rivet is in place on the reverse.

1.4 FASTENERS, TAGS & PINS

Pins and fasteners continued in use during the Late Saxon and Anglo-Norman periods, where they were commonly used to secure the head-coverings and mantles of well-dressed women.

Fig.1.4-a. A graceful, tapering copper-alloy pin with a hinged annular head. The flanking cloisons contain white and yellow enamel fill. Similar finds have been made in the Viking Age levels at Dublin and elsewhere, although the presence of the enamel cells is unusual. It was found in Nottingham and is now in Nottingham Castle Museum.

Fig.1.3-n
(Scale 1.25:1)

a

b

c

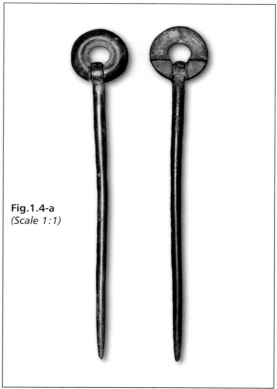

Fig.1.4-a
(Scale 1:1)

Fig.1.4-b
(Scale 1.5:1)

Fig.1.4-b. A copper-alloy domed pin head with animal decoration and a thickened rim. The creatures form into a grotesque face with bulging eyes. From the Kennis collection.

Fig.1.4-c
(Scale 3:1)

Fig.1.4-d
(Scale 1:1)

Fig.1.4-c. A beautifully detailed head from a substantial Norman/Anglo-Scandinavian silver-gilt pin of 10th-12th century date. The top bears an incised circle enclosing a panel of gold foil. Each of the four sides is similarly decorated, but with an inscribed curvilinear lozenge filled with niello. The flattened upper corners bear roundels. The lower face is rounded to meet the shaft of the pin, lost in antiquity. It was found at North Ormsby, Lincolnshire.

Fig.1.4-d. A high status Anglo-Norman copper-alloy dress pin with a long tapering central bar, its decorative surface resembling a horse's mane. The terminals are in the form of Romanesque beast-heads. It was found in Sussex.

1.5 PENDANTS

Pendants continued to form an important part of Scandinavian female dress in the 11th century. The traditional forms remained in use in the Baltic and Scandinavian lands, but are uncommon in western Europe.

Fig.1.5-a
(Scale 1.25:1)

Fig.1.5-a. The classic image of the Anglo-Scandinavian élite in the 10th-11th century, riding a large horse and about to launch a hawk or falcon from his wrist. Hawking had been a popular pastime for the wealthy since the 7th century AD. It is referred to in the opening section of the poem *The Battle of Maldon* where a young English warrior is riding to the battle and lets his hawk fly free – setting aside the idle pursuits of peace in preparation for the grim business of war. This silver pendant is of Baltic origin.

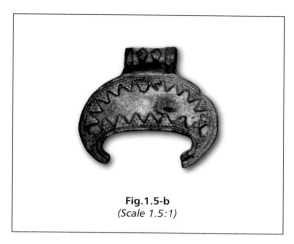

Fig.1.5-b
(Scale 1.5:1)

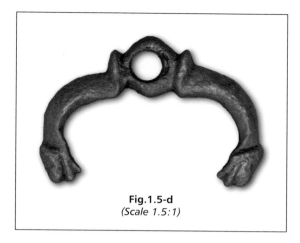

Fig.1.5-d
(Scale 1.5:1)

Fig.1.5-b. Lunulate pendants have a long history in eastern and northern Europe, reaching as far back as the Scythians in the 4th century BC. The present example is formed from flat silver with cast-in added rim and suspension loop. Decoration takes the form of pelleted triangular features and granulation on the face and lozenges on the loop. It is of Scandinavian origin.

Fig.1.5-d. A 10th-12th century cast copper-alloy bifacial lunulate pendant formed as two beasts with sinuous necks attached to a central ring. Each head is formed with a prominent brow and jaw. It was found at Tilbury, Essex.

1.6 MOUNTS

The term 'mount' is used here for a variety of metallic objects which seem to have formed part of the costume or equipment of individuals, perhaps as fittings from a shield, horse-harness, sword-belt or even from a casket or book. The true purpose of many of them will perhaps never be known but they are all decorative and therefore were meant to be displayed.

Anglo-Scandinavian stirrup mounts are considered separately below (section 1.9.1).

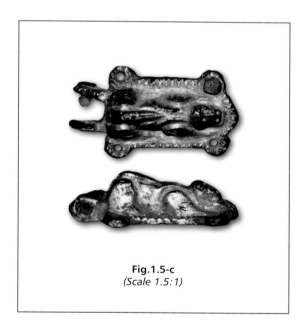

Fig.1.5-c
(Scale 1.5:1)

Fig.1.6-a
(Scale 1.25:1)

Fig.1.5-c. A finely made hinged pendant fitting with a heavily gilded surface, of 11th-12th century date. The central figure is a crouching hound in Romanesque Style with prominent eyes and its tail placed flat along the ridge of its back, hollow-cast in the round. The figure is surrounded by a pentagonal plaque with pelleted border and discoid lobes at four corners, each pierced to accept a tiny fixing rivet, one of which remains in situ with its washer. The upper edge features two circular lugs, pierced for suspension as a hinge and bar, part of which remains. It was found at Hastings, Sussex.

Fig.1.6-a. A cast bronze openwork mount in the form of a central open rectangle with arcaded lateral borders, with a triangular openwork extension. Four spherical knops are located at the corners of the rectangle, with traces of a fifth at the apex of the triangle. The triangle is formed with an internal motif of three bilinear loops forming a knot executed in openwork. The mount is cast with similar decoration on both faces. It was found in Norfolk.

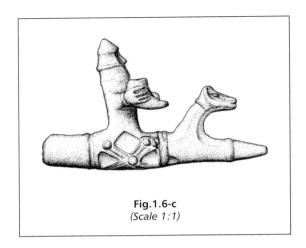

Fig.1.6-b
(Scale 1.5:1)

Fig.1.6-b. A 12th century cast gilded stud mount, convex in profile, with a high relief figure of a rampant griffin with both forelegs extended and wings spread in front of and behind the head, and subtriangular panels around the rear of the body. The gilding extends to the reverse and the remains of a central spigot are visible. The rim bears a scrolled border. It was found at Fakenham, Norfolk.

Fig.1.6-c. A Scandinavian horse-and-rider mount from Charnwood, Leicestershire. It is cast in copper-alloy modelled in the round in the form of a helmeted warrior with a prominent nose and triangular beard, clasping a horn in his right hand. In Anglo-Saxon and Viking tradition, it was customary to offer a noble guest a drink to greet him, and there are references in Norse poetry to the Valkyrie battle-maids who welcomed dead warriors into the hall of *Óðinn* with a horn of mead. Oddly the warrior's legs and saddle are not shown, and the horse is modelled only from the shoulders. A panel of strapwork, similar to the designs on some stirrup-mounts, appears where the lower body should be.

Fig.1.6-d
(Scale 1.5:1)

Fig.1.6-d. An Anglo-Scandinavian mount with four double looped fixings around the rim. The centre of the mount is inlaid with shades of blue cloisonné work; the centre of the inlay is in the shape of a mask with two spirals which form the eyes and brows. The nose is represented by a tear shape with a clearly marked moustache below. The technique is clearly the same as used for the champ-levé disc brooches (section 1.1.1) and the extra provision for fixings implies that it may have strengthened the junction of two straps or belts. It was found in Essex.

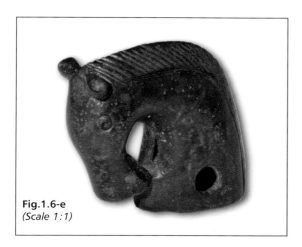

Fig.1.6-e
(Scale 1:1)

Fig.1.6-e. A hollow cast bronze mount in the form of a horse's head with hatched mane, small elliptical ears, ring-and-dot eyes and clubbed muzzle. The socket is elliptical in plan with a large attachment hole to one side. The mount probably formed the decorative finial to a staff and dates from the 11th-12h century AD. It was found near York, Yorkshire.

Fig.1.6-f
(Scale 1.25:1)

Fig.1.6-f. A 9th-11th century Hiberno-Norse cast silver discoid mount with domed central panel and pelletted concentric borders; two holes to the rim for attachment and a central triskele motif. Findspot unknown.

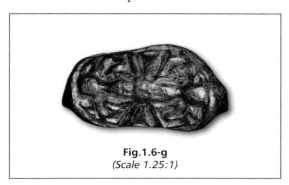

Fig.1.6-g
(Scale 1.25:1)

Fig.1.6-g. A heavy cast belt loop with elliptical front plate and narrow band behind, enabling it to slide on the belt or strap. The chip-carved design comprises a cross pattée

with rounded ends to the upright and an elliptical depression to the ends of the arms. Between the arms are four s-shaped serpentine creatures. The rear bar is sharply angled and rectangular in section. It was found in Norfolk.

Fig.1.6-h
(Scale 1:1)

Fig.1.6-h. A cast bronze mount with Romanesque style leaping beast in high relief. The animal has a forked tail ending in lobes which resemble plant ornament. From the Kennis collection.

Fig.1.6-i
(Scale 1.5:1)

Fig.1.6-i. A slender D-section copper-alloy mount with heavy decoration found at Burnham Market, Norfolk. The upper terminal is shaped as a beast-head with rounded ears, with panels of complex involuted bands below; at about two-thirds of its length there is a slight waist and at the lower terminal a slight bifurcation. The attachment peg on the reverse is rounded over (reminiscent of a raven's head in profile): these features in combination give the piece the appearance of a bird with its wings folded along its flanks and its tail spread. The design - animal masks and fleshy foliage - is similar to later examples of the 10th-11th century Winchester Style.

Fig.1.6-j
(Scale 2:1)

Fig.1.6-j. A rare cast bronze openwork Ringerike Style plate in the form of a rectangular frame containing a complex interlaced zoomorphic panel. The design comprises a large s-curved lupine creature with long muzzle and a spiral hip, facing over its back towards two serpents which encircle the larger animal's hind-legs. Four attachment rivets are still present in the shorter sides. The scene appears to depict the binding of the monstrous wolf, *Fenrir*, one of the dangerous supernatural offspring of the god *Loki*. The gods undertook several attempts at binding the wolf, because they believed it to be a menace to the order of the world, but all the fetters they devised failed; eventually they created a binding from magical, non-existent ingredients (the roots of a mountain, the beard of a woman, etc.) but the wolf refused to allow the gods to place the fetter on him without some form of surety of their good faith. Eventually, the war-god *Tyr* agreed to place his hand in the wolf's mouth as a pledge: the wolf proved unable to break the fetter and was thus captured. All the gods laughed at this except *Tyr*, who lost his hand. When the wolf finally breaks free from his fetter, the ending of the world will ensue. It was found in East Yorkshire.

Fig.1.6-k. An openwork cast D-shaped mount in gilded copper-alloy, with a thick (about 4 mm) border, executed in Winchester Style. The central design is a bird with large, three-toed feet and its neck bowed round so that the bird's beak meets the base and the wings are folded along its flanks. The plate is formed with two piercings to accept attachment rivets, both still in situ. The upper edge is a simple hinge with the three elements still present. The rivets' shanks are about 3.5 mm long and the cleats are still in place. The small distance between the plate and the cleats and the small size of the plate in relation to the hinge suggest that the mount was probably attached to a leather purse or pouch. It was found in East Anglia.

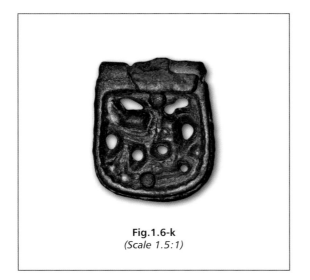

Fig.1.6-k
(Scale 1.5:1)

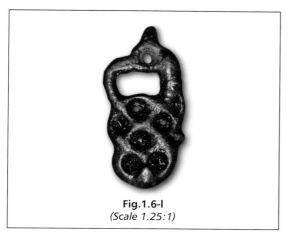

Fig.1.6-l
(Scale 1.25:1)

Fig.1.6-l. A heavy cast openwork copper-alloy mount depicting a beast with open jaws encircling the hole for the attachment rivet, its long slender body curled into an S-configuration and enmeshed in its own lappet, typical of the Urnes Style. The mount is plain and flat on the reverse, with a protective triangular panel at the lower edge, mirrored on the obverse. The Urnes Style appeared in the 11th century, too late to have much influence over mainstream Anglo-Saxon decoration although its effects can be detected in some manuscript illuminations. It was found in Hampshire.

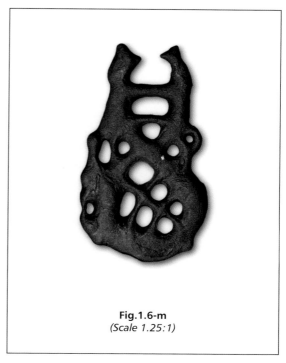

Fig.1.6-m
(Scale 1.25:1)

Fig.1.6-m. A cast Scandinavian Urnes Style openwork mount, cast in D-section copper-alloy with a flat reverse. The design is an 8-shaped animal body amid a tracery of curved tendrils. It was found in Kent.

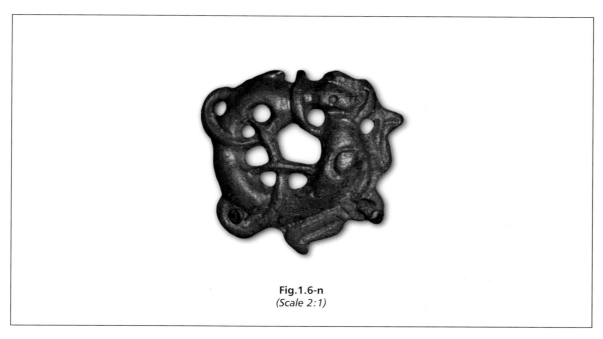

Fig.1.6-n
(Scale 2:1)

Fig.1.6-n. A beautifully cast 11th century openwork mount in the form of a serpentine creature curled into a circle and biting its own tail, with a tracery of thinner tendril legs looped around the body. Two attachment pins are in place, one with the copper-alloy cleat still present. The use of graceful curves and fine tendrils indicates the Late Viking Urnes Style, the last evolution of Scandinavian art before European Romanesque came to dominate. The animal depicted is probably *Jormungandr*, the great monstrous serpent of Viking mythology, which dwells in the sea and will come up onto the land at the end of the world, where it will kill and be killed by the god Thor (*Þorr*). The mount is slightly convex in section, for attachment to a curved surface. The mount was found in Suffolk.

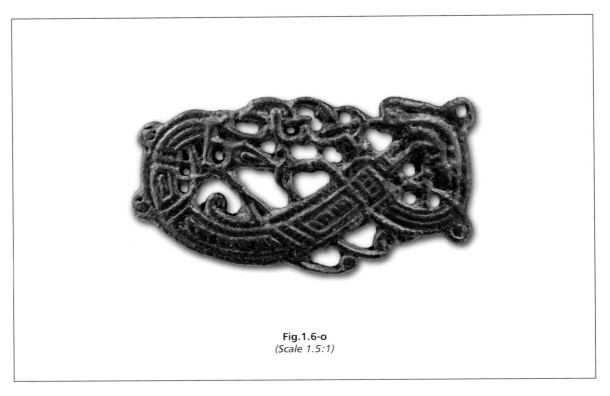

Fig.1.6-o
(Scale 1.5:1)

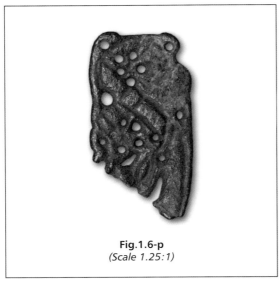

Fig.1.6-p
(Scale 1.25:1)

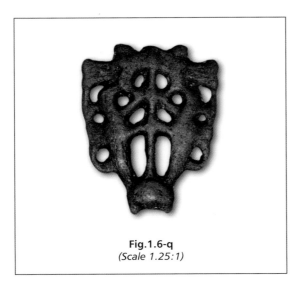

Fig.1.6-q
(Scale 1.25:1)

Fig.1.6-o. A 10th-11th century cast copper-alloy openwork mount in the form of an S-shaped Ringerike Style beast. The body is decorated with panels of hatching interlaced with openwork tendrils with scrolled ends. The tendrils turn at the outer ends to form the frames for the attachment rivets, three of which are present. The design includes elements of the earlier Jelling Style (i.e. hatched body panels) with the later Ringerike Style (i.e. the mesh of tendrils, lentoid eye). It is of Scandinavian origin.

Fig.1.6-p. A cast openwork mount or strap end with convex sides featuring a serpentine creature executed in Urnes Style, the sinuous body enmeshed in a network of fine tendrils. It was found in Suffolk.

Fig.1.6-q. A good example of Anglo-Scandinavian bifacial openwork casting craftsmanship. The design features two opposed beasts whose muzzles converge at the top, forming a stylised animal-mask. This design, the so-called Nordendorfer Motif, is a feature of Germanic art through the Merovingian, Anglo-Saxon and Viking periods, and derives ultimately from details of Roman military hardware. It was found in Suffolk.

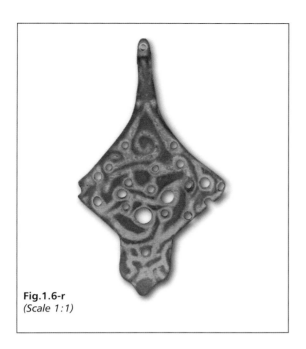

Fig.1.6-r
(Scale 1:1)

Fig.1.6-t
(Scale 3:1)

Fig.1.6-r. An 11th century cast copper-alloy mount formed as a lozenge with elongated neck and broad upper extension. The central panel bears a design in an Anglo-Scandinavian version of the Urnes Style, featuring a beast and serpent entwined, executed in openwork with the head extending onto the narrow neck, pierced about 1.5 mm from the end. It was found at High Garrett, Essex.

Fig.1.6-t. A 10th-11th century cast copper-alloy fitting in the form of an animal's head with pierced lobes above the hollow ears. The fitting is U-shaped in section and D-shaped in plan, with a prominent median ridge for the nose and annular ridges for the eyes. The fitting seems to have been designed to accept a pair of cords or thongs through the upper holes and to cover the point where they were spliced into a thicker band. The design of the face is similar to a series of disembodied beast-head elements found in the decoration of manuscripts from the later 10th and 11th centuries, incorporating both Carolingian and Scandinavian influences. It was found in Wiltshire.

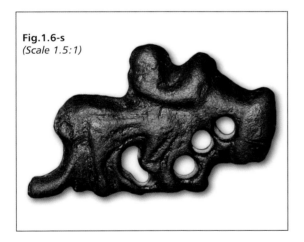

Fig.1.6-s
(Scale 1.5:1)

Fig.1.6-u
(Scale 1.5:1)

Fig.1.6-s. This figural openwork mount features a horse and rider, cast in thick copper-alloy which allows for very rounded modelling of the subject. There are traces of inlay in the area of the horse's eye and bridle. The rider appears to have a horn raised to his lip, and his leg and stirrup are clearly moulded. The horse's rear end develops from a foliate motif which evidently formed the attachment ring. The style is more naturalistic than is usual in Viking art, and may show the influence of Romanesque Style features on Anglo-Scandinavian design. It was found in Kent.

Fig.1.6-u. An 11th century gilt-bronze mount in the form of a standing beast with tilted head. The execution of the design recalls aspects of Norman period stone sculpture in which an animal is depicted in a formal and stylised manner. The gilding was executed with a high degree of craftsmanship, but due to extensive abrasion it remains only in the incised design features including the lateral strokes of the fur texture. There is an attachment lug to the reverse. It is from a Surrey collection

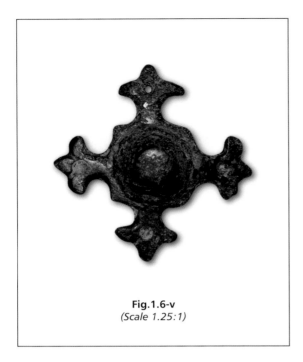

Fig.1.6-v
(Scale 1.25:1)

Fig.1.6-w
(Scale 1.25:1)

Fig.1.6-v. A Norman or Anglo-Scandinavian quatrefoil domed fitting comprising a central cone emerging from a square base, from each edge of which projects a fleur-de-lys shaped lug pierced to accept an attaching rivet. It may have been part of the decoration of a horse's bridle or harness at the junction of two straps and was found in Norfolk.

Fig.1.6-w. A hollow-cast bronze mount in the form of a human bust. The hair is indicated by a raised panel with several series of incised lines. The brow and nose form a single element framing tear-shaped eyes, and the mouth is a transverse slit. The upper body is covered by a cloak with a fringed border which falls from the right shoulder across the chest. It was found in Yorkshire.

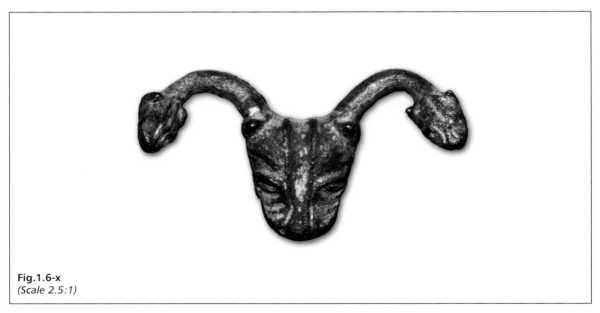

Fig.1.6-x
(Scale 2.5:1)

Fig.1.6-x. A cast gilt copper-alloy mount of 11th-12th century date in the form of a Romanesque Style beast-head with curved extensions. The mount is D-shaped, its flat underside provided with a sturdy attachment peg, formed as an animal's head with small triangular ears, a central ribbed panel running over the top of the head terminating at the muzzle with lentoid extensions to the eyes. The muzzle features two small indented nostrils above the slightly open mouth with tongue. From each upper corner emerges a D-section C-shaped horn ending in a miniature version of the larger head. It was acquired in London in 1994.

Fig.1.6-y
(Scale 1:1)

Fig.1.6-y. A finely detailed domed bronze openwork mount, discoid with slots to the left and right edges, possibly to accept a strap running to the reverse. The central motif is a coiled serpentine creature enmeshed in a vineleaf design within a border of vegetation with incised running vinescroll and segmented outer edge. Four holes to the inner edge were for the attachment rivets. It is of 12th century date. From the Kennis collection.

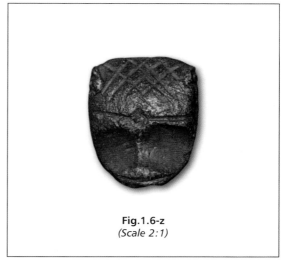

Fig.1.6-z
(Scale 2:1)

Fig.1.6-z. A 12th century cast copper-alloy mount in the form of a stylised animal head with broad cross-hatched forehead, D-shaped ears, two concave recesses with a central ridge and broad muzzle detail on the lower edge. The reverse is cast hollow with the remains of an integral attachment rivet still in place. It was found in Staffordshire.

Fig.1.6-aa. A 12th century Norman period cast gilt-bronze beast mount depicting an advancing bird, possibly a swan, with a human face on a recurved neck supporting a crown or frieze of tufted feathers. The head wears a coif or tight-fitting headdress. The wing is cross-hatched and the neck textured with punched point detailing; the feet are webbed, standing with a single foot on a decorated pedestal base. The frieze is pierced for attachment pins. It was found in South Yorkshire.

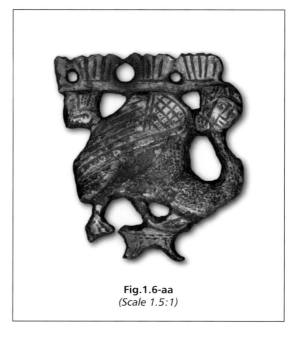

Fig.1.6-aa
(Scale 1.5:1)

1.7 RINGS, ARM-RINGS & BRACELETS

Finger rings remained a popular dress item, with some fine examples known. They were among the badges of office of leading clerics and royalty. Arm and neck rings continued in use among the Scandinavians where they acted as a display of wealth.

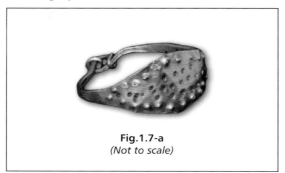

Fig.1.7-a
(Not to scale)

Fig.1.7-a. A Viking finger ring formed as a single lozengiform sheet. The flat hoop expands to a broad bezel with repoussé roundels along the outer edges and rows of punched-point detailing in the middle. The ends of the hoop are twisted about each other. Findspot unknown.

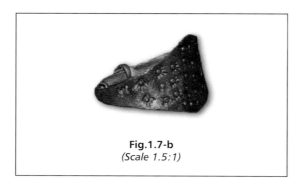

Fig.1.7-b
(Scale 1.5:1)

Fig.1.7-b. A sheet bronze finger ring formed as a lozenge with overlapped ends coiled; the centre decorated with columns of stamped decoration. It was found at Winteringham, Humberside and dates from the 9th-11th century AD.

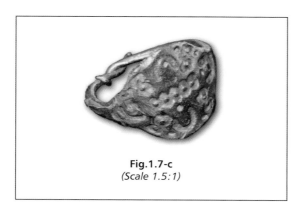

Fig.1.7-c
(Scale 1.5:1)

Fig.1.7-c. A 10th-11th century gold finger ring comprising a large discoid bezel with lateral round-section extensions, the ends twisted around each other to form the hoop. The bezel is decorated with punched motifs comprising a central horizontal band of rings with reserved central pellets, with further pairs of these punchmarks placed in the north-east, south-east, south-west and north-west quadrants. Deep C-shaped horseshoe punchmarks are placed facing inwards above and below the central band of rings, and at the ends of the band. Additional punched-point pellets are placed below the inner arc of each horseshoe and around the perimeter of the bezel. It was found at Tostock, Suffolk.

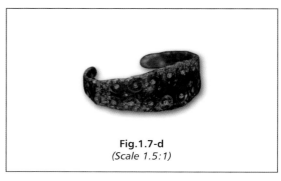

Fig.1.7-d
(Scale 1.5:1)

Fig.1.7-d. A good example of a Middle-Saxon or Anglo-Scandinavian finger ring formed as a lozenge-shaped band, the wider part forming the bezel and decorated with punched ring-and-dot motifs along the outer edges. Similar simple forms of finger ring were used by the Vikings in the eastern Baltic (Lehtosalo-Hilander's Group 14 from the Luistari Viking period finds). It was found in Norfolk.

Fig.1.7-e
(Scale 1.5:1)

Fig.1.7-e. A 10th-11th century finger ring formed from thick (1 mm plus) copper-alloy sheet cut as a broad central section and narrowing ends. The widest section bears two ring-and-dot designs aligned vertically, with two more to one side and three to the other. Between the ring-and-dot motifs are series of elongated incised marks forming a border. It was found in Suffolk.

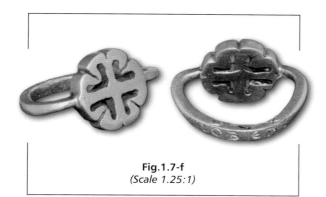

Fig.1.7-f
(Scale 1.25:1)

Fig.1.7-f. An Anglo-Norman or later gold cast finger ring, D-shaped in profile. The bezel is in the form of a cross moline with openwork detail to the centre forming a cross. The ring bears the name 'Robert' in majuscule to the outer face of the hoop and 'Dux' on one lateral face. It was found in Hampshire.

Fig.1.7-g. A substantial finger ring of Viking or Anglo-Scandinavian type comprising an expanding cast band with modelled spiral detailing, imitating the classic form of expanding twisted wire rings from Scandinavia. It was found in Derbyshire.

Fig.1.7-h. A 9th-1th century AD finger ring formed from plaited gold wire, forged together behind and each end coiled around the other. Findspot unknown.

Fig.1.7-i. A rare type of copper-alloy finger ring with a single-band shank dividing in two at each end, and the ends forming two pairs of tight opposed spirals in an openwork design. It is of Baltic origin.

Fig.1.7-j. A decorative silver finger ring formed as a rod with a wide, flat centre decorated with filigree and granulation. The narrow ends are drawn out and looped round the shank, making the size of the ring adjustable. It is of Baltic origin.

Fig.1.7-k. A Baltic Viking ribbed finger ring of Lehtosalo-Hilander's Type III. The central rib is D-sectioned. The decoration on the flanges consists of punched tremello-style (zigzag) vertical linear bands. The shank is a continuation of the central rib and extends to form a thin rod at each end which runs back round the finger to create a three-band effect. It is of Baltic origin.

Fig.1.7-g
(Scale 1.25:1)

Fig.1.7-h
(Scale 1.25:1)

Fig.1.7-i
(Scale 1.25:1)

Fig.1.7-j
(Scale 1.25:1)

Fig.1.7-k
(Scale 1.5:1)

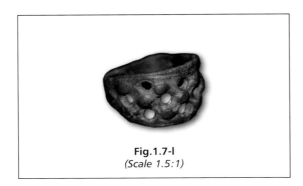

Fig.1.7-l
(Scale 1.5:1)

Fig.1.7-l. A carefully crafted copper-alloy expanding-band finger ring made in the strap-and-boss style of the Anglo-Scandinavian stirrup strap-mounts of Class A Type 12, with openwork decoration consisting of circular piercings and diagonal straps with bosses at the junctions. The strap-and-boss motif was a common means of decorating plain surfaces in later 10th and 11th century Scandinavian metalwork, occurring also on tortoise brooches, dress pins and elsewhere. It is of Baltic origin.

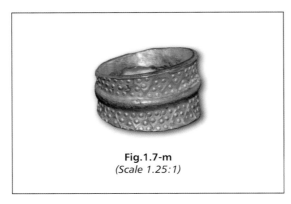

Fig.1.7-m
(Scale 1.25:1)

Fig.1.7-m. A 10th-11th century AD cast gold annular finger ring with expanding hoop and raised median band, the outer face impressed with punchmarks, each a triangle with pellets in the corners. It is from an important West Yorkshire collection.

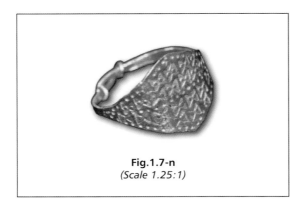

Fig.1.7-n
(Scale 1.25:1)

Fig.1.7-n. A fine gold finger ring formed in one piece with a plain band and integral lozengiform bezel with stamped decoration. The punchmark is in the form of the rune *dæg*,

the character 'd', which stood for the life-giving properties of the dawn in Anglo-Scandinavian and Viking tradition. The bezel has a pelletted border. It was found in continental Europe and dates from the 9th-10th century AD.

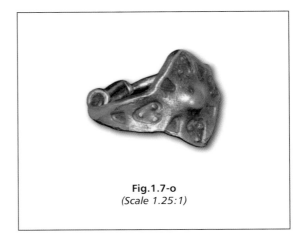

Fig.1.7-o
(Scale 1.25:1)

Fig.1.7-o. A gold finger ring formed as a lozengiform bezel with central boss surrounded by punched decoration, four triangular, four chevrons with three pellets, triangular punchmarks on the shoulder; the hoop formed as extensions of the shoulder looped around each other. It is from an old European collection and dates from the 9th-11th century AD.

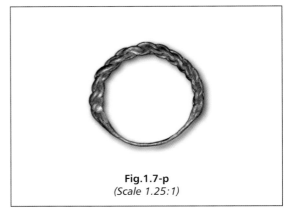

Fig.1.7-p
(Scale 1.25:1)

Fig.1.7-p. A fine example of a Hiberno-Norse finger ring in which the majority of the hoop is formed from three wires of about 1 mm diameter plaited into a band; the lower portion is a single wire of the same type. There is a similar gold wire ring from Ardtrea (County Tyrone, Ulster) in the National Museum of Ireland, Dublin. It is from an American collection.

Fig.1.7-q. A 9th-11th century AD gold finger ring formed with a plain bar lower hoop, the upper divided into three expanding rods and twisted. It is from a European collection.

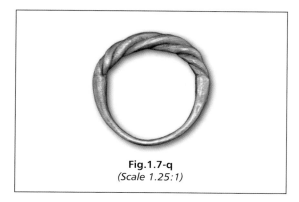

Fig.1.7-q
(Scale 1.25:1)

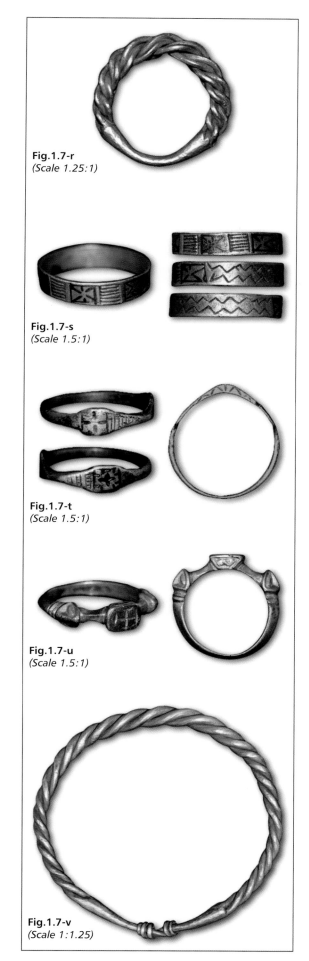

Fig.1.7-r
(Scale 1.25:1)

Fig.1.7-s
(Scale 1.5:1)

Fig.1.7-t
(Scale 1.5:1)

Fig.1.7-u
(Scale 1.5:1)

Fig.1.7-v
(Scale 1:1.25)

Fig.1.7-r. A Hiberno-Norse gold finger ring formed as an expanding plait in three bands each of two gold rods, developing from a solid shank. This method of manufacture is typical of Scandinavian workshops in the Viking period; the plaited structure provides some elasticity. It was formerly part of the David Clements collection.

Fig.1.7-s. A beautiful decorated silver band of 11th-12th century date, the underside of the ring is detailed with a double zigzag pattern that terminates half way up each side. The shoulders are detailed with three box sections that enclose stylised cross motifs filled with niello, separated by two boxes containing rows of six incised lines. It was found in Continental Europe.

Fig.1.7-t. A beautiful 11th/12th century AD stirrup-shaped ring with decorated shoulders and pointed bezel. The shoulders splay out from the shank in square section then taper into a point at the bezel; each is decorated with a different style cross to the other with niello inlay, the first has a cross with square boxed arms and a small cross in the centre, the other is made up from four lines disconnected at the centre. Both sides of the pointed bezel are detailed with small incised lines. Findspot unknown.

Fig.1.7-u. A silver-gilt finger ring with two stylised animal heads similar to those on Norman mounts and buckles. It has a sub-rectangular bezel carved with a cross potent, with two trapezoidal panels either side each carved with a beast facing back. Either side of the bezel are flat shoulders gripped by stylised heads, probably serpentine, triangular and with lentoid eyes. Findspot unknown.

Fig.1.7-v. A bracelet formed with twisted expanding gold rods, the closure formed with the ends twisted round each other. It dates from the 9th-11th century and is from a European collection.

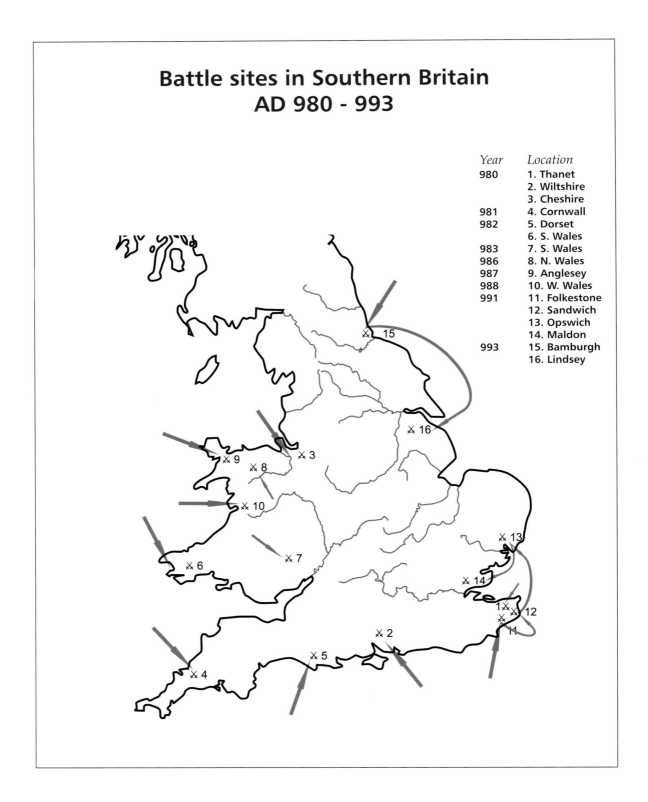

**Battle sites in Southern Britain
AD 980 - 993**

Year	Location
980	1. Thanet
	2. Wiltshire
	3. Cheshire
981	4. Cornwall
982	5. Dorset
	6. S. Wales
983	7. S. Wales
986	8. N. Wales
987	9. Anglesey
988	10. W. Wales
991	11. Folkestone
	12. Sandwich
	13. Opswich
	14. Maldon
993	15. Bamburgh
	16. Lindsey

1.8 WEAPONS & MILITARY EQUIPMENT

Weapons from Anglo-Scandinavian England are not a common find, although there are several examples of swords and axes from the period elsewhere in Europe. Weapons were prized badges of honour and, as Christians were not allowed to take them to the grave, they probably remained in use for generations.

Not all types of weapons would survive: we know from the poem *The Battle of Maldon* that 'bows were busy' at the beginning of the fight, but small arrowheads are easily overlooked. Likewise, the Bayeux Tapestry shows Bishop Odo and some other combatants fighting with wooden clubs.

1.8.1 Swords

The sword remained the most prized weapon of the age, and the one with the greatest symbolic value. Some examples included a great deal of decoration on the hilt, allowing the owner to display his wealth and fine taste. Norman swords were generally longer and heavier than the Anglo-Saxon and Viking examples, with a plain disc or brazil-nut pommel. The lower guard lengthened so that it formed a classic cross-shaped profile.

The practice of depositing swords, spears and knives in flowing water, which had been used intermittently since at least the Bronze Age, appears to have continued into Late Saxon times with many examples known mainly from the rivers of eastern England. While there has been speculation that these finds might relate to battles fought at fords and bridges in the Viking period, there is mounting evidence to show that many were deposited as offerings in a tradition which is known from Britain and Scandinavia. (The tradition may have continued with pilgrim badges being deposited in water in later medieval times.)

Fig.1.8.1-a. An iron sword, the hilt fittings decorated with carefully inlaid silver strips in the surface of the bronze matrix to both pommel and guard. The pommel is of Petersen's Type H and of 10th century date. It is from a private collection.

Fig.1.8.1-a
(Not to scale)

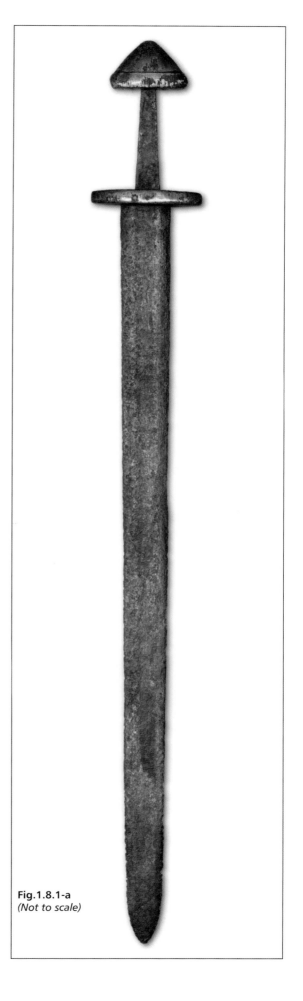

Fig.1.8.1-a
(Not to scale)

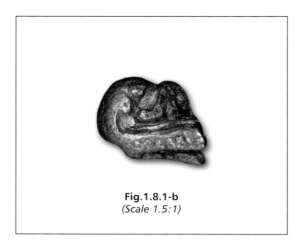

Fig.1.8.1-b
(Scale 1.5:1)

Fig.1.8.1-b. The terminal of a silver-gilt Viking sword pommel, probably of Petersen Type O or R, of later 10th century date. The pommels of swords of these types consist of a wide, relatively thick casting with three heavy medial lobes and decorative, often zoomorphic, terminals. The piece has been cast with an angled aperture to accept the attachment rivet. The decoration consists of a stylised bird-of-prey head cast in the round with bulbous eyes and its beak modelled as a three-lobed coil. The beak features incised line and punched pellet detailing; the neck which develops into the pommel-cap is decorated with a ropework panel; further ropework detailing is present on the underside. Gilding remains in the recessed areas. The practice of splitting up high-status metalwork is a recognised custom among Viking Age societies - sometimes for purposes of recycling, but often as part of the division of spoils of war. It is from an old English collection.

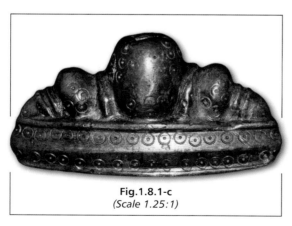

Fig.1.8.1-c
(Scale 1.25:1)

Fig.1.8.1-c. A robust and very substantial cast copper-alloy sword pommel from the later 10th or 11th century AD. The integral cross-guard consists of two outer horizontal ribs and an inner carinated panel bearing two rows of ring-and-dot decoration. The pommel consists of a large medial lobe, elliptical in plan and in section, decorated with ring-and-dot motifs in

quincunx formation; this is flanked by two smaller but similar lobes set at a slightly oblique angle and similarly decorated. Between these three elements are raised carinated bands. Further carinated bands extend beyond the outer edges of the smaller lobes, and the rounded finials bear a single ring-and-dot on each face. The pommel is pierced vertically to accept the tang, in a long rectangular profile at the bottom rising to a square profile at the top. The lower edge of the pommel is slightly inward-curved. The pommel is similar in profile and layout to the example found in a lake near Søborg Castle, Denmark; there are several other swords of this type including the fine example from the famous Viking grave at Gjermundbu (Norway). On the finest swords, the upper guard and interstitial bands carry silver filigree. It is from an American collection.

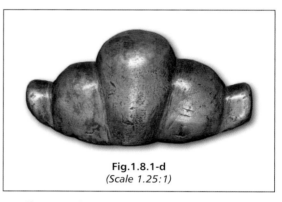

Fig.1.8.1-d
(Scale 1.25:1)

Fig.1.8.1-d. A cast silver sword pommel cap formed with three bulbous lobes and two flared finials, of Petersen's Type S. It is of late 10th-early 11th century date and Scandinavian origin.

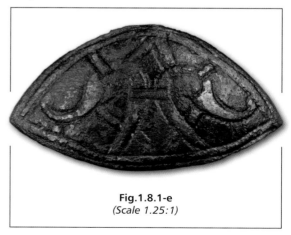

Fig.1.8.1-e
(Scale 1.25:1)

Fig.1.8.1-e. An 11th century cast bronze brazil-nut sword pommel, hollow to the underside and with a hole above for the tang. It is decorated on each face with a panel of Ringerike Style ornament. It was found in Nottinghamshire.

Fig.1.8.1-f. A Viking or Anglo-Scandinavian seven-lobed bronze sword pommel of 10th century date. The hollow-cast pommel is formed as five parallel lobes and two horn finials. The central lobe is pierced by a longitudinal circular hole though which the blade's tang passed. The profile is consistent with the curved guards of Petersen's Type L hilts, a form found in Scandinavia (i.e. the Korsøygarde sword) derived from Anglo-Saxon forms (i.e. the Abingdon sword). It was found at Fakenham, Norfolk.

Fig.1.8.1-g. A rare cast bronze pommel of Type S, of 10th century date. The pommel is cast hollow with a hole for the tang to pass through at the top and is divided into five separate lobes with plain channels between; the outer lobes feature incised Mammen Style coiled leaf designs; the median lobes feature stepped key design; the central lobe features a pair of addorsed coiled tendrils on one face and Mammen Style meshed tendril motif on the other. At each end on the underside an integral peg extends to attach the pommel to the upper guard of the hilt. Originally, the channels were filled with silver wire ropework, contrasting with the yellow sheen of the bronze. It was found in Lincolnshire.

Fig.1.8.1-h. A sturdy, cast copper-alloy lower guard from the hilt of a Viking period sword of the 10th-11th century. The guard is elliptical in plan, with a large (58 mm x 9 mm approx.) opening in the underside to accommodate the upper end of the blade, and a smaller rectangular (15 mm x 7 mm approx.) slot in the upper face to accommodate the tang. The guard is cast hollow in the centre. The front and rear faces are decorated with a series of incised scrolled designs with silver wire inlay, similar in layout to the work on the guard of the Viking period sword from Kilmainham (Eire) and on swords from Malhus and Korsøygarden (both Norway). It was found in Hampshire.

Fig.1.8.1-i. A late 10th or 11th century sword with a narrow blade and central fuller along most of its length. The lower guard is curved downwards – a feature found on Anglo-Saxon swords of the 9th and 10th century – but the pommel is stylistically closer to Petersen's type S with it large medial rounded lobe and two smaller flanking lobes. It is from an American collection.

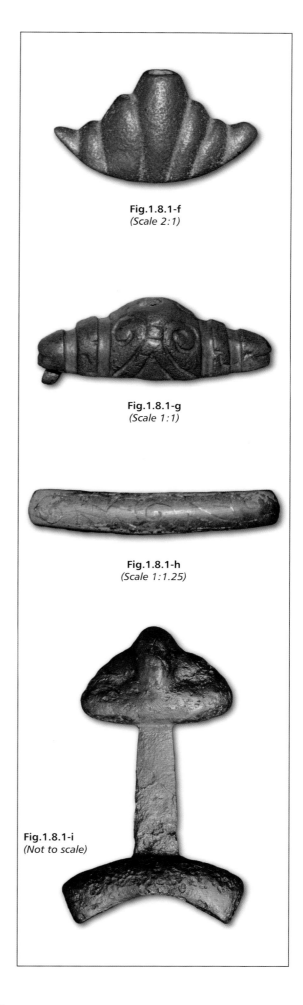

Fig.1.8.1-f
(Scale 2:1)

Fig.1.8.1-g
(Scale 1:1)

Fig.1.8.1-h
(Scale 1:1.25)

Fig.1.8.1-i
(Not to scale)

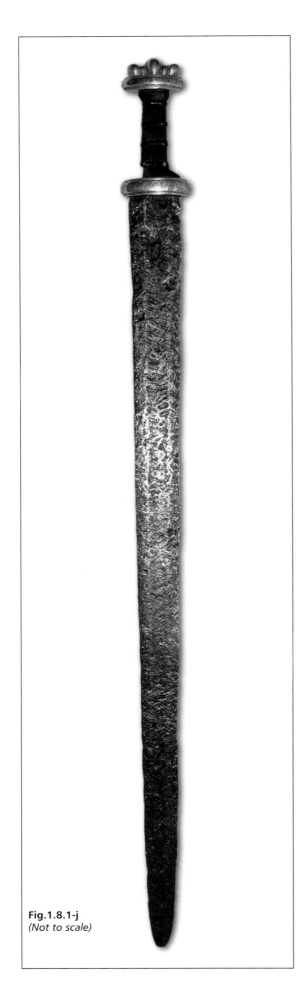

Fig.1.8.1-j
(Not to scale)

Fig.1.8.1-j
(Scale 1:1)

Fig.1.8.1-j. A later 10th century sword of remarkable workmanship with lenticular-section straight guards, three-lobe Type T pommel with plain interstitial bands and pattern-welded blade. The pommel and guards have silver casings decorated with ring-and-dot and vertical bar motifs placed regularly around the perimeter. The original rectangular-section bone grip is present, with four carved transverse ribs to assist with handling the weapon efficiently in combat. The blade is parallel-sided with a rounded, flat-section point and single broad fuller to each face. The surface of the blade shows the results of the pattern-welding process with the characteristic herringbone effect to the centre and sheer, chamfered edges of the steel outer shoe. The quality of the workmanship and the generous

66

use of silver for the fittings indicate that the owner was both wealthy and important: there are parallels in the hilt of a sword found at Kilmainham, Ireland (now in the National Museum of Ireland, Dublin) and another in the Statens Historiska Museum in Stockholm, Sweden. It is a Scandinavian find.

Fig.1.8.1-k. A hand-forged iron sword comprising a long, narrow and gently tapering blade, round-section crossguard with flared and clubbed finials, flat-section tang and brazil-nut pommel. The blade is provided with a shallow fuller to both faces and the tip is slightly rounded. It was found in Continental Europe.

Fig.1.8.1-l. A finely-crafted Viking period sword of the 9th-10th century AD with a thin (about 3 mm) blade and long (110 mm) grip. The hilt is of the unusual Petersen's Type I, a later 9th century form which continued in use up to the middle of the 10th century. The pommel is sub-triangular in profile with an elliptical cross-section, and with a noticeable step where the rounded upper element connects to the flatter upper guard. The pommel and guard are unusually thin for a Viking period sword. The tang is broad and flat, and shows the continuation of the bars which form the pattern-welded blade. The lower guard is about 90 mm wide, flat and slightly elliptical in cross-section with a broad rectangular slot for the blade and tang. The blade is about 55 mm wide at the maximum, composed from two twisted iron billets and an outer shoe: the billets have been created from blocks of iron of varying grades, twisted and forge-welded to each other, then thinned and stretched to the length of the blade (presently 81 cm). The outer edges were formed from a single billet of steel, split and forged onto the core. The surface treatment shows very clearly the construction method and the characteristic herringbone pattern created by the opposed twist of the central billets. The process of pattern-welding was practised in northern Europe from the early centuries AD up to the end of the Viking age, producing very striking surface effects which were much prized. It is a Scandinavian find.

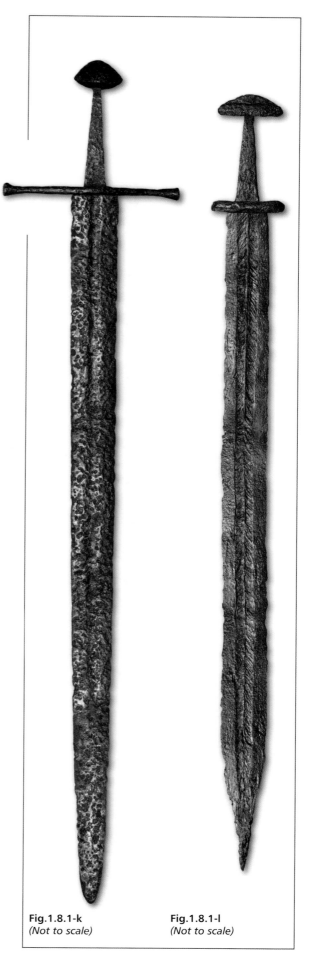

Fig.1.8.1-k
(Not to scale)

Fig.1.8.1-l
(Not to scale)

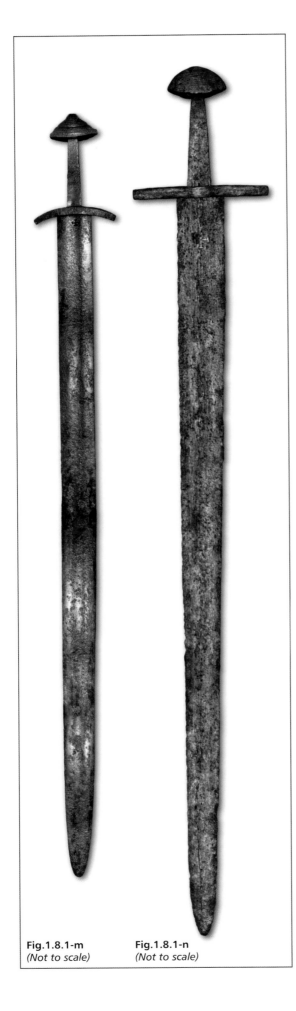

Fig.1.8.1-m. An iron 'Type L' hilted sword of 10th century date with 75 cm long hand-forged iron blade, lentoid in section with a distinct central fuller, gently tapering to a rounded tip. The outer ends of the guard are curved steeply towards the blade, elliptical in plan and rectangular in section. The (antler, bone or wood) grip is lost and the tang is flat in section, tapering towards the upper end. The upper guard below the pommel is less sharply curved and the three-lobe pommel is rounded in profile; on one face of the upper blade below the guard is a stamped cross potent with second cross-stroke to one arm. It was found in Cornwall.

Fig.1.8.1-n. An 11th century iron hand-forged sword with a Type X 'brazil nut' pommel and lenticular square-section crossguard. The blade is gently tapered with a shallow flat-section central fuller, the blade's piled construction is visible in the core. There are three inlaid brass crosses potent below the hilt. The use of religious symbolism on weapons was an important tradition of long standing in northern Europe and was adapted for use by devotees of the Christian religion. It was found in Continental Europe.

Fig.1.8.1-m
(Not to scale)

Fig.1.8.1-n
(Not to scale)

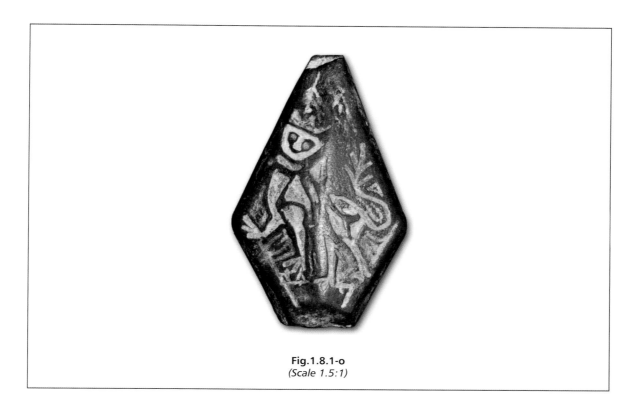

Fig.1.8.1-o
(Scale 1.5:1)

Fig.1.8.1-o. A beautiful 12th-13th century cast copper-alloy sword pommel of Oakeshott's Type F, lozengiform in profile and facetted in section. The two main faces are decorated with champ levé enamelled motifs: to one face, two human figures flanking a tree and to the other a lion rampant gardant crowned. It was found at Ely, Cambridgeshire.

Fig.1.8.1-p. A wheel-type 12th century pommel with twelve serrations, enamelled heraldic designs on both sides. One face has a red outer circle enclosing a crowned lion coloured in red, white and blue enamel; the other has the same outer circle enclosing a griffin coloured with blue and red enamel. Both areas outside of the circle show traces of blue enamel. It was found in Essex.

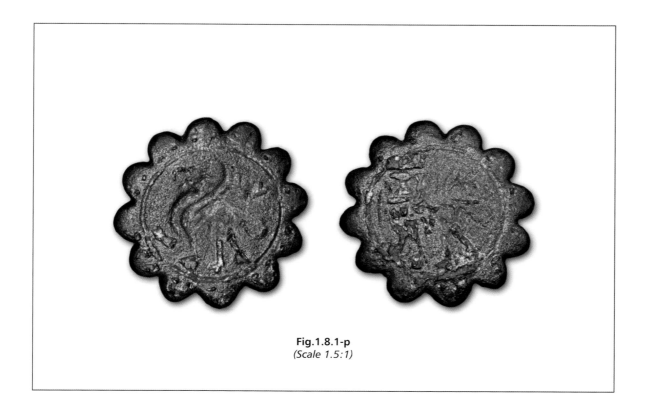

Fig.1.8.1-p
(Scale 1.5:1)

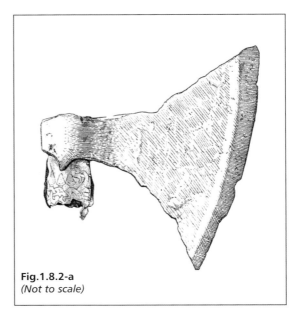

Fig.1.8.2-a
(Not to scale)

1.8.2 Axes

Axes became an increasingly important weapon in the Late Saxon period, and their use against horsemen is clearly shown in the Bayeux Tapestry where heavily armoured infantrymen wield them to great effect. The warriors depicted on the Bayeux Tapestry are shown with similar equipment, but the large, curved axe is unique to the English forces.

Fig.1.8.2-a. An iron axehead with curved profile and thickened section just behind the cutting edge for better penetrating power.

1.8.3 Spears

Anglo-Saxon and Viking spears in the Late Saxon Period apparently retained the same basic leaf-shaped profile with lentoid section as had been in use since the Early Saxon period. Spears were the most important offensive weapon, even if not the most costly, and every warrior had to be proficient in their use.

Fig.1.8.3-a. A narrow, lozenge-section spearhead with a long socket ornamented with inlaid silver wire in the tauschierung technique also used on sword grips (see 1.8.1-a). It is from an American collection.

Fig.1.8.3-b. A classic socketted spearhead with slight median rib to the blade. The socket is gilded with a reserved Urnes style serpentine design. It is from an American collection.

Fig.1.8.3-c. A spearhead similar in profile to 1.8.3-b with gilded socket and two reserved serpents enmeshed in circumferential bands. It is from an American collection.

Fig.1.8.3-a
(Not to scale)

Fig.1.8.3-b
(Not to scale)

Fig.1.8.3-c
(Not to scale)

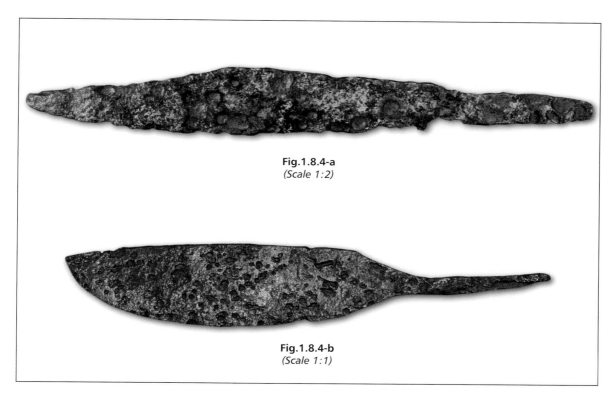

Fig.1.8.4-a
(Scale 1:2)

Fig.1.8.4-b
(Scale 1:1)

1.8.4 Knives & Daggers

Knives and daggers were used as handtools as well as weapons. They were mainly made by blacksmiths working in the local tradition.

Fig.1.8.4-a. A forged iron blade from a seax, a type of knife used for hunting and in war. The blade is slender with a slightly inward-curved forward edge and a distinct change of angle on the rear, referred to in the literature as the 'broken-backed' profile, Wheeler's Type II/III. The scooped forward edge provides a narrow point for thrusting. The tang is 8 cm long, broad and flat-sectioned, and was inserted into a horn, bone or antler sleeve to form the grip. The knife is short in the blade and sturdy, perfect for use in a shieldwall clash where there was no room to swing an axe or sword. It was found at Barrington, Cambridgeshire.

Fig.1.8.4-c
(Scale 1.25:1)

Fig.1.8.4-b. A standard form of early medieval iron knife, formed as a broad triangular-section blade with a shallow curvature where the edge rises to meet the back, and narrowing to a spiked tang for insertion into a wooden, antler or horn handle. This blade-shape remained in use into the later medieval period, but with the more common scale-tang which was held between two wooden or antler plates and riveted. The spiked tang on this example suggests an Anglo-Norman date, possibly 12th century AD. It was found in Hertfordshire.

Fig.1.8.4-c. A slotted copper-alloy knife pommel of Late Saxon or Norman provenance. The elongated bulbous terminal extends to a rectangular panel, into the underside of which is inserted a rectangular slot. The edges bear cast incised lines; one of the broad faces bears three columns of ring-and-dot decoration, while the other features a saltire with ring-and-dot motifs in the quadrants. The two piercings are in one face only, suggesting that the pommel was pinned to a solid surface, probably the wooden or bone handle of a knife. It was found in Kent.

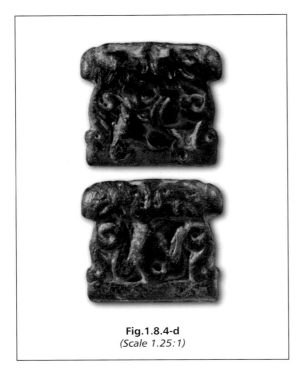

Fig.1.8.4-d
(Scale 1.25:1)

Fig.1.8.4-d. A cast bronze pommel, flat in section, with a collar to the mouth and broad upper face. The sides are decorated with reserved scrollwork and the upper face with a cross within foliage. It is of Late Saxon or Norman date, 11th-12th century AD and was found in Essex.

1.8.5 Scabbard Fittings

Late Anglo-Saxon and Anglo-Scandinavian fittings are often very substantial castings in bronze, with Winchester Style or Ringerike Style decoration executed in openwork to reveal the contrasting colour(s) of the leather beneath. No convincing example of a Middle or Late Saxon scabbard slide has been found in England, although Cameron notes that remains of leather scabbards from Gloucester and York bore the clear impressions of these: they were probably made from antler or bone and have not survived.

Fig.1.8.5-a. A 10th-11th century cast bronze openwork belt fitting with three voids and knotwork central panel; attached to one void a cast bronze zoomorphic strap end in openwork with attachment rivets to the rear. It was found in continental Europe.

Fig.1.8.5-b. An openwork scabbard chape of later 10th century Baltic Scandinavian type, executed in Mammen Style with gripping beast motifs and a central animal mask – compare the animal masks on Class B Group 8 stirrup mounts of 11th century date. It was found in Gotland.

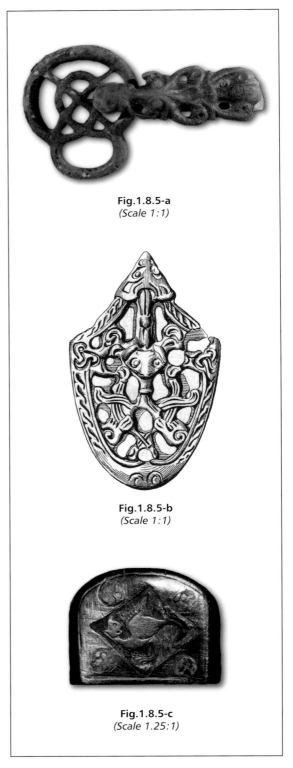

Fig.1.8.5-a
(Scale 1:1)

Fig.1.8.5-b
(Scale 1:1)

Fig.1.8.5-c
(Scale 1.25:1)

Fig.1.8.5-c. A Romanesque Style figural scabbard chape with incised lozengiform panels on the back and front, one depicting a griffin with a raised wing looking back to its right, the other a stylised two-legged beast looking back to its right. Traces of silver inlay remain in the fields of each face. Around both panels are four quatrefoils with silver inlay remaining. There is a cross-hatched design around the edges with a border containing more silver inlay. It was found in Essex.

Fig.1.8.5-d
(Scale 2:1)

Fig.1.8.5-d. A 12th century cast copper-alloy rectangular plate with a recess to the left edge and attachment holes on the upper and lower right edge. The design features a stylised figure facing, with a spear in the right hand and teardrop shield in the left, with nasal helmet and square panels on the flared armoured coat. The field is heavily keyed for champ-levé enamel. Acquired in London in 1981.

THE CHAPES RESEARCH PROJECT

The subject of Anglo-Norman dagger chapes has been studied by Peter Woods and colleagues at the Chapes Research Project; their findings have been published as series of occasional articles in *The Searcher* magazine from 2006 onwards and are summarised here. The defining characteristic of this small group of chapes is that they are made by casting a thin sheet and folding it over one edge of the knife's sheath; the design accommodates the folding process and attachment rivets, and produces a broadly symmetrical effect on each face. Woods's initial classification was into three classes, each with sub-groups and variants. The principal types are:

Type 1 – zoomorphic with squared end, horse with triangular projection to the back

Type 2 - zoomorphic with squared or pointed end, other animal than a horse

Type 3 – triangular with pointed end

Type 'Anglo-Scandinavian' – zoomorphic, club-shaped end

On both Types 1 and 2 the folded edge of the chape extends along the flat edge of the sheath while the slightly curved outer edge may have a short bar extension with a pierced disc at the end to accept the securing rivet.

The imagery of Type 1 chapes sometimes includes a rider; if the horse is intended to be the winged horse Pegasus, as Woods suggests, then the rider ought to be Bellerophon who rode such a winged horse in his hunt for the chimaera.

However, the discovery of an 'Anglo-Scandinavian' group in the northeast, of a generally heavier construction than elsewhere, suggested a possible source in Norse tradition, perhaps based on the horse-and-rider motifs seen on mounts such as item 1.6-s on p.55. Woods's further research suggested a link to Romanesque imagery derived from Byzantine representations of St. Michael.

Distribution of Anglo-Norman Chapes & Fittings

● Findspots of
Chapes & Fittings
(after Woods)

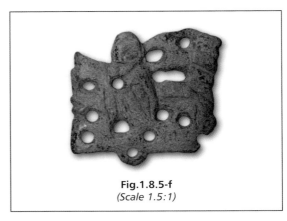

Fig.1.8.5-f
(Scale 1.5:1)

Fig.1.8.5-f. An openwork copper-alloy Type 1B mount, probably from a sword's scabbard, in the form of a helmeted figure with one prominent eye; the crest of the helmet is shown as a separate band which runs into the nasal. The figure is seated on a horse, whose head is placed in front of the figure's chin. A series of vertical strokes suggests a riding cloak is placed around the horseman's body. The horse's rump bears a horizontal bar, perhaps intended for the crupper of the harness. A zoomorph behind the rider's back is probably intended to represent a falcon. Beneath the horseman is a pierced lobe for attachment. It was found in Norfolk.

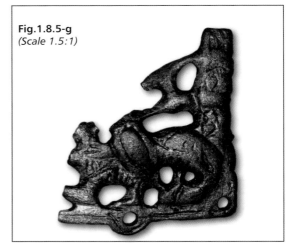

Fig.1.8.5-g
(Scale 1.5:1)

Fig.1.8.5-g. A detailed copper-alloy chape or scabbard mount (Woods's Type 1B – zoomorphic or 'Pegasus' form) from a high status sword, depicting a mounted horseman brandishing a large axe. The horse stands on the base with a wide detailed border rising up from the corner. This border joins the hind of the horse and the axe, terminating interlocking vines. Below the axe can be seen the large elliptical shaped Norman tear-drop shield resting on the side of the horse. (The upper part of the horseman and the horse's head are missing.) It was found in Cambridgeshire.

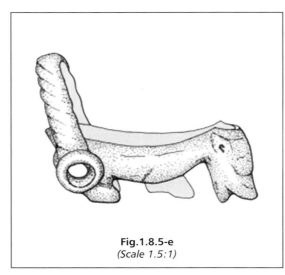

Fig.1.8.5-e
(Scale 1.5:1)

Fig.1.8.5-e. An example of Type 3Biii showing the zoomorphc side panels and attachment loop formed from the ropework tail. It was found near Bungay, Suffolk.

Fig.1.8.5-h
(Scale 1.5:1)

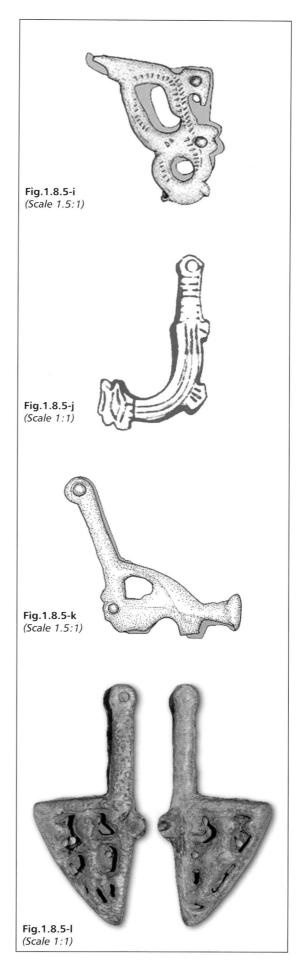

Fig.1.8.5-i
(Scale 1.5:1)

Fig.1.8.5-j
(Scale 1:1)

Fig.1.8.5-k
(Scale 1.5:1)

Fig.1.8.5-l
(Scale 1:1)

Fig.1.8.5-h. A triangular openwork copper-alloy mount with cast decoration, probably the chape from a decorated leather scabbard for a sword or hunting knife (Woods's Type 3B). The decorative scheme consists of a panel of converging longitudinal lines on each outer face, interrupted by a tear or shield-shaped panel, with an openwork recess on the lower edge and a corresponding one on the upper: through these the tooled and coloured leather of the sheath could be seen. The triangular shape and plain panel can be interpreted as an animal-head. The narrowness of the object and the sharply triangular shape suggest a knife rather than a larger item such as a sword. It was found near York, Yorkshire.

Fig.1.8.5-i. A Type 2Cii sub-triangular in profile with large openwork animal-head at the lower end. The lateral surfaces are textured with punchmarks. It was found at Amesbury. Wiltshire.

Fig.1.8.5-j. A rare J-shaped chape of Woods's Type 2Ei with ribbed surface to the lateral plates and a ribbed collar above It was found in Exeter, Devon.

Fig.1.8.5-k. A triangular chape of Woods's Type 2Bii with extension bar to the rear. It was found in Hampshire.

Fig.1.8.5-l. An 11th century cast openwork dagger-sheath chape (Type 3B) formed as two triangular panels with openwork designs and arms extending to the rear. To one face of the chape, a stylised horseman with outstretched arms; to the other a stylised bird, an eagle, hawk or falcon. The arms with lobes, pierced to accept securing rivets, still in place. It was found in Cambridgeshire.

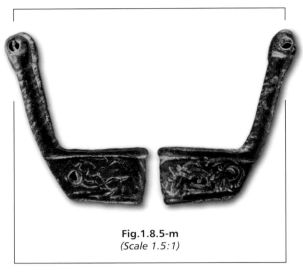

Fig.1.8.5-m
(Scale 1.5:1)

Fig.1.8.5-m. A 10th-11th century cast copper-alloy mount for a knife's sheath. The mount comprises a u-shaped band and two arms. The band is decorated with dense Winchester Style vegetation ornament, and the arms with ropework. The ends of the arms are pierced to accept an attachment rivet, and there is a hole for another close to the junction of the arms and band. The gap in the folded band is about 3 mm, just enough to accommodate a slender knife and fine leather sheath, attached along the seamed edge for protection. There are parallels to this format in the array of rivets and plates applied to the edge of the seax in Grave 65 at Donzdorf, Baden-Wurttemberg, Germany. It was found in Buckinghamshire.

Fig.1.8.5-n
(Scale 1.5:1)

Fig.1.8.5-n. A cast bronze scabbard or sheath mount (Woods's Type 3B) depicting a helmetted horseman with teardrop shield on a caparisoned horse, with an axe over his shoulder; one of two ribbed arms to the rear of the rider. It was found in Hampshire.

Fig.1.8.5-o
(Scale 1.5:1)

Fig.1.8.5-o. A cast bronze openwork dagger sheath fitting in the form of an L-shaped border with figure of a mounted knight in a helm amid foliage (Woods's Type 3B). There are attachment points in the corner of the border and pierced lug below the horse. It is from a County Durham collection.

Fig.1.8.5-p
(Scale 1.5:1)

Fig.1.8.5-p. A figural chape fitting of Woods's Type IB dating from between circa AD 1080 and 1200 featuring a hunter facing to the right bestriding his prey, a hart with elaborate antlers. The casting features details of the woodland setting, with the hart's body placed in front. This scene is found on a number of these Norman chapes and evidently had great importance for the owners; often, on the reverse was a horseman in full combat array, showing the two prime aspects of Norman male aristocratic life: war and hunting. It was found at Tilbury, Essex.

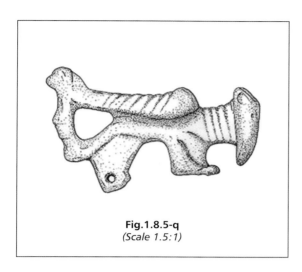

Fig.1.8.5-q
(Scale 1.5:1)

Fig.1.8.5-q. A winged beast with folded head (the other face lost). This form is described as 'Anglo-Scandinavian', Woods's Type 2Ai. It was found in North Yorkshire. (After Woods)

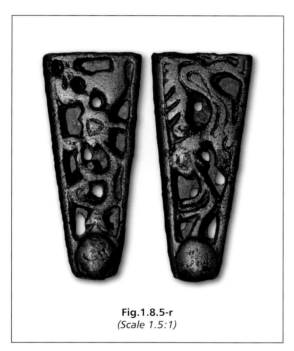

Fig.1.8.5-r
(Scale 1.5:1)

Fig.1.8.5-r. A finely detailed openwork chape for a medieval dagger sheath, cast in copper-alloy. One face is decorated with a quadruped with open mouth, its curling tongue extending the length of the frame and its bushy tail brought over its back to touch the back of its head. The other face features a smaller quadruped with its feet on the upper border of the chape and its head tilted back, with a long, forked, curling tongue protruding from its open mouth. The lower ends of both faces are strengthened with hemispherical bulbs, each bearing an animal mask with D-shaped ears placed above a broad brow. The side-faces are plain and rectangular; the end of

the chape is open. The execution of the animals is consistent with Romanesque Style, although the design appears to have remained in use after the Norman period and unlike the majority of 11th-12th century Anglo-Norman chapes, it was not designed to be folded over the wood-and-leather frame of the sheath. It was found in Norfolk.

Principal Castles in the 11th Century

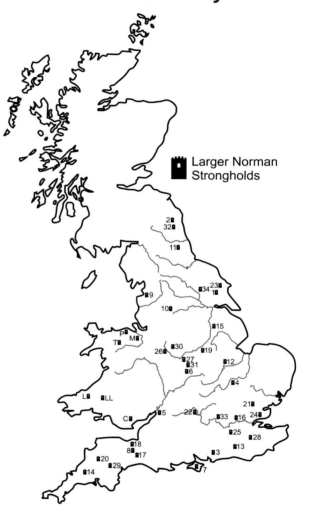

■ Larger Norman Strongholds

1 Acklam Castle	17 Montacute
2 Alnwick Castle	18 Nether Stowey
3 Arundel Castle	19 Nottingham Castle
4 Bedford Castle	20 Okehampton Castle
5 Berkeley Castle	21 Ongar Castle
6 Brinklow Castle	22 Oxford Castle
7 Carisbrooke Castle	23 Pickering Castle
8 Castle Neroche	24 Rayleigh
9 Clitheroe Castle	25 Reigate Castle
10 Dudley Castle	26 Stafford Castle
11 Durham Castle	C Cardiff Castle
12 Fotheringhay Castle	L Lampeter Castle
13 Lewes Castle	LL Llandovery Castle
14 Launceston Castle	M Mold Castle
15 Lincoln Castle	P Prestatyn Castle
16 London (Tower)	T Tomen Castle

1.8.6 Maceheads

Maces and other blunt trauma weapons such as cudgels were always a popular side-arm in medieval armies. The cast metal heads survive in some numbers but they are seldom closely datable.

Fig.1.8.6-a
(Scale 1:1)

Fig.1.8.6-a. A robust bronze casting comprising a long tubular socket with narrow collar and three rows of pyramidal spikes. Mounted on a short haft, the mace formed an impressive weapon for delivering blunt-trauma injuries. It was found near Castle Hedingham, Essex and dates from the 12th-13th century AD.

Fig.1.8.6-b
(Scale 1:1.5)

Fig.1.8.6-b. A cast copper-alloy macehead, formed to accept a shaft of about 26 mm. The upper end bears a series of twelve spikes (eleven remaining), the upper and lower rows of D-section and the middle row of lozenge-section. A thick collar below secures the mace head to the wooden shaft, with a hole to accept an attachment pin. It was found in Sheffield.

Fig.1.8.6-c
(Scale 1:1)

Fig.1.8.6-c. An important cast macehead with inlaid silver decoration within triangular panels. Scandinavian origin, dates from the 12th century AD.

Fig.1.8.6-d
(Scale 1:1.5)

Fig.1.8.6-d. A 12th-14th century iron macehead with lozengiform panels to the exterior. It was found in Cambridgeshire.

Fig.1.8.7-a
(Scale 1:1.5)

1.8.7 Helmets & Armour

Helmets and defensive armour were to develop rapidly in the Late Saxon period. The Danish warriors who accompanied King Cnut were called *húskarlar* (young men of the household) and this tradition was taken over as the Late Saxon 'housecarls', who traditionally fought with broad axes used with two hands. Standardised forms of helmet, shield and mailcoat are shown on the Bayeux Tapestry.

Fig.1.8.7-a. A Norman-style four-plate riveted conical helmet fabricated from triangular iron sheets, skilfully made to accommodate the curvature of the human head and with a knop at the apex. The plates are contoured so that the front and back plates overlap the side-plates by 1-2 cm; iron rivets pass through this overlap to secure them in position. The rivets are worked flat into the surface of the helmet, and are almost invisible from the outside but can be detected on the inner surface. The inverted lower rim is furnished with an additional series of rivets to accommodate a lining. There are two protruding rivets at the base of each side-plate, where the cheek-plates were originally attached. The plate-junction at the apex is closed off with the inserted knop.

Helmets of this general profile and with some form of plume or other crest are a long-lived military fashion. The riveted-plate construction is known across Europe from the Migration Period (5th entury AD) through to the 12th century. It is from eastern Europe.

1.9 RIDING EQUIPMENT

Riding was one of the favoured pastimes of Anglo-Saxon and Norman lords, who loved hunting as a sport as well as a means of keeping their strategic skills sharp in readiness for war. No less was riding a necessity for merchants, officials, leading churchmen and others whose careers involved responsibility for a large territory.

1.9.1 Stirrup Mounts

Stirrup mounts are a distinctive class of cast copper-alloy artefacts which formed part of the decorative display on Anglo-Scandinavian horse-gear. The mounts are usually triangular or lozengiform, with a sharp ledge at the rear of the lower end and a hole to accept a rivet at the upper end; in use, the apex was riveted to the stirrup-leather which passed upwards to the saddle, while the lower end was riveted to the uppermost loop of the stirrup itself. The current typology is that of David Williams, published in 1997; the large number of metal-detected finds which have appeared since the book appeared mean that the system is in need of revision. Outside England, the mounts are found in Scandinavia, Germany and the Netherlands, which supports the association with later Viking activity around the North Sea rim. The decoration shows Ringerike Style elements, and there are a few mounts which appear to be influenced by Urnes Style: these two facts indicate a date-range of circa AD 1020 to 1050 for their use, with some areas maintaining them up to about AD 1100. It is tempting to link their introduction into England with the increased Danish influence under King Cnut (AD 1016-35), but more detailed study will have to be undertaken before any such proposal can be advanced seriously.

Stirrup Mount Distribution

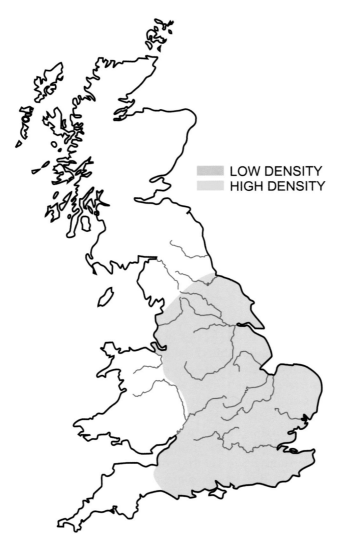

LOW DENSITY
HIGH DENSITY

Fig.1.9.1-a
(Scale 1:1)

Fig.1.9.1-a. An 11th century AD cast stirrup mount of Williams's Class A (Unclassified) bearing serpentine decoration on its tongue-shaped outer surface. The creature's body is formed as a loop with its head emerging from the lower edge between the rivet-holes. Piriform elements are set adjacent to the top piercing. The head is snub-nosed with D-shaped ears and almond-shaped eyes. The rear ledge is of the right-angled type and the profile of the mount is a gentle s-curve. It was found in Suffolk, England.

Fig.1.9.1-b
(Scale 1:1)

Fig.1.9.1-b. A finely cast example of an 11th century 'Class B, Type 4' mount formed as a plate with a beast's head in relief with triangular muzzle and staring eyes. The edges are scalloped, which Williams considers to be typical of East Anglian examples. The rear ledge is complete with its two rivets still present as a ferrous accretion. The upper edge features a central lobe, pierced to accept a rivet. From the Kennis collection.

Fig.1.9.1-c
(Scale 1:1)

Fig.1.9.1-c. A remarkable stirrup mount of the 'male-face' type with finely modelled features and protruding lentoid eyes, triangular nose and a neat moustache. From the Kennis collection.

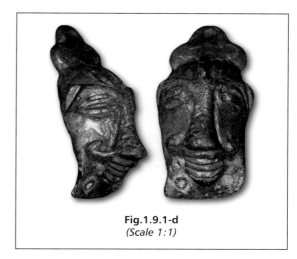

Fig.1.9.1-d
(Scale 1:1)

Fig.1.9.1-d. The more ornate forms of stirrup mount were moulded in the half-round to give spectacular effects. The present example is a human mask, full of character with smiling mouth and neatly curled moustache. It is of Williams's Class B Type 4, the so-called 'East Anglian face mounts'. It was found in Norfolk.

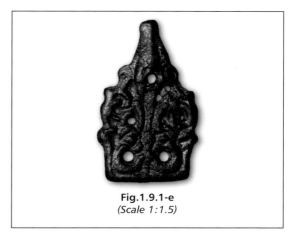

Fig.1.9.1-e
(Scale 1:1.5)

Fig.1.9.1-e. A flat openwork stirrup mount of Williams's Class A Type 2. The wolf-head detail at the top has been placed prominently above the rivet-hole for the suspension strap, and the ears of the wolf develop into serpentine creatures along the outer edge of the mount. It was found in Norfolk.

Fig.1.9.1-f
(Scale 1:1)

Fig.1.9.1-f. An 11th century cast copper-alloy stirrup mount of Williams's Class B Type

3 Group 1. The triangular upper section is ribbed on the outer edges and the main plate bears a moulded bear's head with openwork ears. The flange on the rear of the lower edge is rivetted to the remains of the bracket. It was found near Eye, Norfolk.

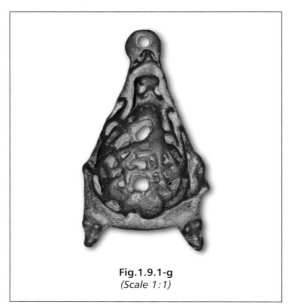

Fig.1.9.1-g
(Scale 1:1)

Fig.1.9.1-g. A cast copper-alloy stirrup mount of Williams's Class A (unclassified). The fine Urnes Style interlaced pattern is executed in openwork on the domed surface. It is from an American collection.

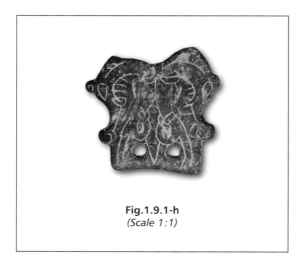

Fig.1.9.1-h
(Scale 1:1)

Fig.1.9.1-h. A mount of Williams's Class A Type 1 characterised by a pentagonal profile and incised decoration. The ornamentation consists of two addorsed pendant animal heads with long, drooping necks and enmeshed tendrils influenced by the Scandinavian Urnes Style. The lower field between the two rivet holes features an openwork section formed from the beasts' bodies. The upper loop was lost in antiquity. It was found in Cambridgeshire.

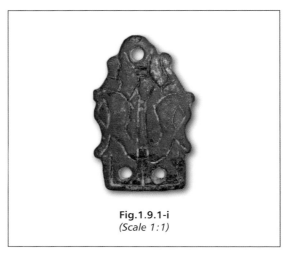

Fig.1.9.1-i
(Scale 1:1)

Fig.1.9.1-i. A Class A Type 1 stirrup mount with incised decoration – two addorsed dragon-heads hanging from a central column. It was found in Hertfordshire and dates from the 11th century AD.

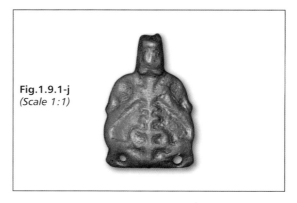

Fig.1.9.1-j
(Scale 1:1)

Fig.1.9.1-j. An example of Williams's Class A Type 6 of 11th century date. The central column with spiny extensions is the main feature, and the addorsed animal heads on the shoulders have become more like Winchester Style acanthus-leaf features. It is from an American collection.

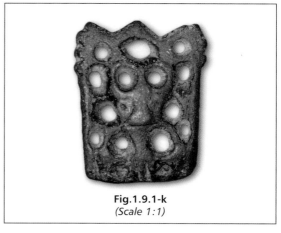

Fig.1.9.1-k
(Scale 1:1)

Fig.1.9.1-k. A finely cast example of the unusual Class B Group 8 mount formed as an openwork plate with symmetrical placement of circular holes. The central figure is an animal mask with staring eyes and triangular nose, surrounded by a network of tendrils. The upper edge is formed as three triangles, with scalloped detailing to the outer corners. The lower flange is a very shallow curvature to the bottom edge, pierced with two rivet-holes in which there are traces of iron residue; a series of vertical grooves is placed between these holes. It was found in Norfolk and dates from the 11th century AD.

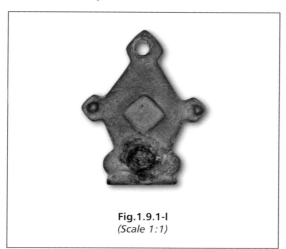

Fig.1.9.1-l
(Scale 1:1)

Fig.1.9.1-l. A lozengiform stirrup mount with decoration consisting of a basic strap-and-boss design. This simple but appealing geometric motif occurs on several 11th century Anglo-Scandinavian object types, and is found in a more evolved form on other stirrup mounts. It is of Williams's Class A Type 13. It was found in Essex.

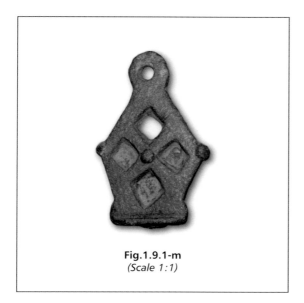

Fig.1.9.1-m
(Scale 1:1)

Fig.1.9.1-m. An 11th century Class A Type 12 mount with internal strap-and-boss decoration on the main field. It was found in Cambridgeshire.

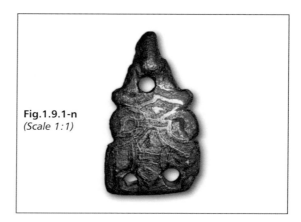

Fig.1.9.1-n
(Scale 1:1)

Fig.1.9.1-n. A rare form of stirrup mount with inlaid silver ornamentation. It is of Williams's Class A Type 1; the decoration is geometric, but follows the general outline of the large human mask on Type 9 mounts. It was found in Continental Europe.

Fig.1.9.1-o
(Scale 1:1)

Fig.1.9.1-o. A crisply cast example of Williams's Class B Group 3. The central beast-head with rounded ears and scaphoid eyes is very clearly depicted against the openwork background which forms a pair of flanking beasts. It was found in Norfolk.

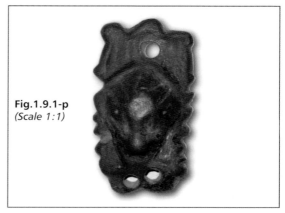

Fig.1.9.1-p
(Scale 1:1)

Fig.1.9.1-p. An unambitious stirrup mount of Williams's Class B Type 4 cast in copper-alloy, with a human mask in the half-round as the only decorative feature. The single hole at the top and double holes in the flange are asymmetrically placed and clearly visible. It is from an American collection.

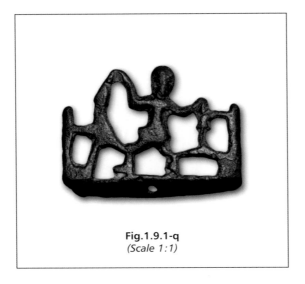

Fig.1.9.1-q
(Scale 1:1)

Fig.1.9.1-q. An interesting openwork stirrup mount showing a human male advancing, his right hand placed above the jaws of a dog which has placed its legs on the left side of the mount's frame. Behind a smaller animal is shown attached to the man's left hand. It is possible that the man is a huntsman with his hounds, or else the smaller animal is a hare or other prey which the huntsman and his hound have caught. The flange beneath forms the base of the scene, and the hole for the attachment rivet is still present. A hunting scene would be an appropriate subject for a piece of riding equipment. It was found in Suffolk.

Fig.1.9.1-r
(Scale 1.5:1)

Fig.1.9.1-r. An 11th century Class A Type 12 mount with internal strap-and-boss construction, rivet holes to the front face and lines of fine punched triangles. It is from an American collection, found Norfolk.

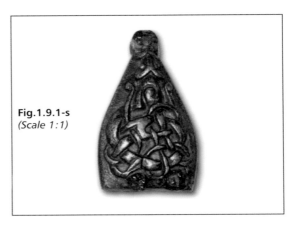

Fig.1.9.1-s
(Scale 1:1)

Fig.1.9.1-s. A piriform stirrup mount of Williams's Class A Type 2. The design is executed in high-relief and features a serpentine creature with interlaced body, the head placed below the attachment loop. It was found in Suffolk.

Fig.1.9.1-t
(Scale 1:1)

Fig.1.9.1-t. A cast copper-alloy terminal with clear beast-head detailing. It is hollow to the underside to accept the edge of the stirrup. It dates from the 11th century and was found in Hampshire.

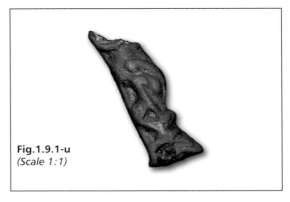

Fig.1.9.1-u
(Scale 1:1)

Fig.1.9.1-u. Apart from the stirrup mount itself, there were additional cast components in the stirrup assemblage. The hollow-backed terminals were fixed on either side of the stirrup at the lower edge, where the sides turn to meet the footplate. This example is decorated with sinuous curved lines in Ringerike style, suggesting a beast advancing with its jaws wide. It was found in Snettisham, Norfolk.

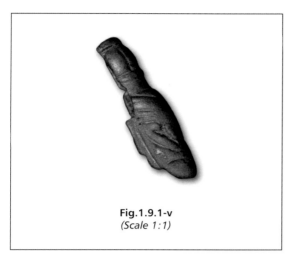

Fig.1.9.1-v
(Scale 1:1)

Fig.1.9.1-v. A finely-made 10th-11th century hollow mount in the shape of an animal-head. A ribbed bulb sits between two plain collars extending to a ribbed brow with lobed, recurved banding forming the eye-socket. The muzzle is delimited by a shallow bulb. The mouth is moulded as an underslung stepped section. The style of the ornamentation is reminiscent of the animal-head detailing of the late 10th century *Ramsey Psalter* and the sculptured stone animal-head from Deerhurst (Gloucestershire). The mount is evidently a stirrup terminal, with the hollow back section attached to the solid mouth and muzzle. It was found in Haverhill, Suffolk

1.9.2 Harness and Bridle Mounts

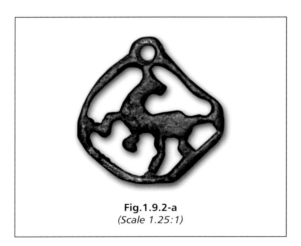

Fig.1.9.2-a
(Scale 1.25:1)

Fig.1.9.2-a. An 11th-12th century openwork cast bronze pendant with integral suspension loop. The discoid frame surrounds a regardant rearing horse connected to the frame at the tail, rear leg, foreleg and ear. Images of rearing animals were popular in Middle Saxon art and remained in the artists' repertoire into the Later Saxon and Norman periods. It was found in Lincolnshire.

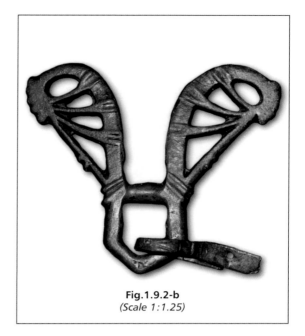

Fig.1.9.2-b
(Scale 1:1.25)

Fig.1.9.2-b. An elegantly designed 10th-11th century Hiberno-Norse cheek piece from the bridle of a horse. The assemblage comprises a single openwork casting for the cheek piece and a separate looped fitting for the reins. The looped fitting is a substantial D-section curve extending to two flat plates, pierced to take an attachment rivet. The junction of the loop and plate is decorated with geometric detailing and a facetted section. The cheek piece comprises a pair of addorsed serpentine heads with elaborate lappets which extend in a radiating series from the crest of the head across the void to rejoin the neck where they bifurcate. The lower lappet in each series bears two transverse ribs towards the lower end. Similar ribs mark the point where the necks join the D-shaped lower hoop to which the loop fitting is attached. The decorative plan is reminiscent of the Viking Ringerike Style which is found on some items from the recent Dublin excavation. It was found in Hertfordshire.

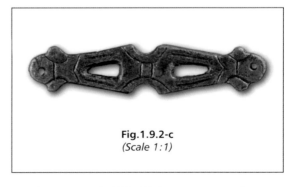

Fig.1.9.2-c
(Scale 1:1)

Fig.1.9.2-c. A 10th-11th century cast bronze openwork symmetrical strap fitting with tri-lobed ends and punched-line segment decoration. It was found in Dragonby, Lincolnshire, UK in 1990.

Fig.1.9.2-d
(Scale 1:1)

Fig.1.9.2-d. An important cast bronze Viking harness pendant of 11th century date, formed as two wolves chasing each other; probably representing the celestial wolves Skoll and Hati who chase the sun and moon. It was found at Thetford, Norfolk.

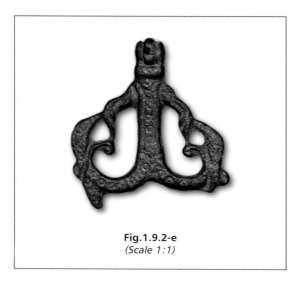

Fig.1.9.2-e
(Scale 1:1)

Fig.1.9.2-e. An early 11th century large horse pendant with two dragon heads, their necks developing from a central downward facing stem, recurved. From each dragon's head a column of flame reconnects to the stem. Ring-and-dot decoration runs down the central body towards the mouths of each dragon. The 'hinge' is typically Scandinavian in form, with two fixing bars, one either side of the hanger – this configuration is the opposite of medieval construction. It was found in Lincolnshire.

1.9.3 Stirrups

Stirrups made in iron with decorative surfaces are a relatively late introduction to Anglo-Saxon England. While a few examples of iron spurs are known from early Anglo-Saxon graves, no early stirrups have ever been detected. This is probably due to the fact that the early versions of this group of items were organic – the word 'stirrup' is from Old English *stige rap* 'climbing rope', indicating that they were made from vegetable material or perhaps leather. By the 8th century, the Franks were using metal stirrups, but the English may have continued with leather (and wood?) for another century or more.

The few examples of high-status stirrups found in England probably date from the mid-11th century and relate to the Scandinavian taste for stirrup loops made in iron; they may have been introduced by the warriors of Cnut.

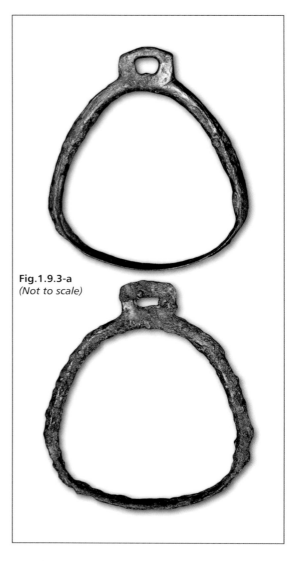

Fig.1.9.3-a
(Not to scale)

Fig.1.9.3-a. A pair of iron stirrups of late Viking Age date. The suspension loop is rectangular with a central trapezoidal slot. The bow is curved in profile, elliptical in section and facetted. The tread is curved, developing in an arc from the lower edge of the bow; on the underside is a slight lip on the edges and a median ridge. They are of Baltic origin.

Fig.1.9.3-b
(Not to scale)

Fig.1.9.3-b. An iron stirrup with inlaid copper-alloy decoration in the form of bands and running spirals, one of a pair found on the banks of the River Cherwell, Oxford. The bars are D-section, with bulbs at the junction with the footplate and suspension loop.

1.9.4 Spurs

Spurs were an essential piece of equipment for horsemen, and several finely-made examples have been found.

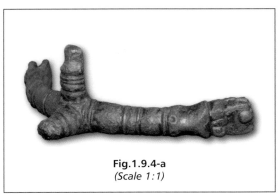

Fig.1.9.4-a
(Scale 1:1)

Fig.1.9.4-a. A cast bronze Anglo-Saxon prick spur of crescent form and D-section with split ends for rivetting to leather straps; the rivets are still present. The body of the spur is balustered with a small central riser; there is animal-head detail at each end, with a central collared socket for the iron pricket. This is a rare example of the type of spur used in East Anglia in the Middle and Late Saxon period

before Scandinavian fashion became prevalent; one of only five recorded examples. It was found near Gooderstone, Norfolk, UK; see Portable Antiquities Scheme record number SF4685.

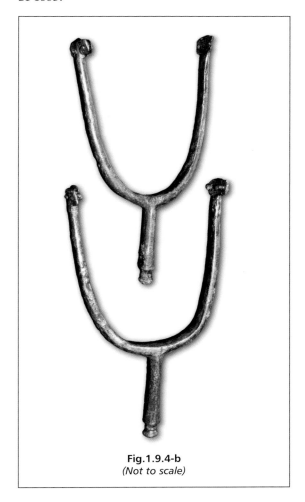

Fig.1.9.4-b
(Not to scale)

Fig.1.9.4-b. A pair of Carolingian Frankish iron prick-spurs of 9th-10th century date, with U-shaped straps, the prickets with domed balustered ends. They were found on the Continent.

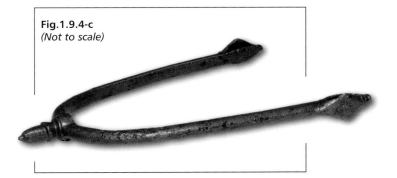

Fig.1.9.4-c
(Not to scale)

Fig.1.9.4-c. An 11th century Late Saxon or Norman prick-spur with a long U-shaped bow and looped sockets with lozengiform outer plates. The short pricket has a collar to the rear. It was found in Suffolk.

Fig.1.9.4-d
(Scale 1:1)

Fig.1.9.4-d. A 10th-11th century AD cast prick spur comprising a C-shaped D-section bow with bulb terminals and conical pricket to the rear with ribbed collar. The outer surfaces of the bow and terminals are inlaid with fine strips of copper and silver wire in the Tauschierung technique. To the rear of the bow is a median panel with inlaid vinescroll motifs. The spur shows Continental workmanship and is from a Canadian collection.

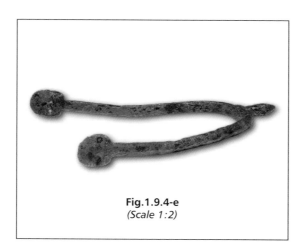

Fig.1.9.4-e
(Scale 1:2)

Fig.1.9.4-e. An iron prick spur with D-section shank and discoid terminals. There are attachment rivets to the inner face and the pricket is rectangular-section with a pointed end. It dates from the 12th century and was found in Lancashire.

1.9.5 Horseshoes

Fig.1.9.5-a
(Scale 1:1.25)

1.9.5-a. A 10th-12th century AD forged iron horseshoe of elongated arched plan with raised stops to the ends. A series of six rectangular piercings to accept the nails are placed close to the outer face, resulting in a wavy outer edge. The style and form of horseshoes varies little in the early medieval period, but the wavy edge disappears in the 13th century AD. It was found at Chepstow Castle, Wales.

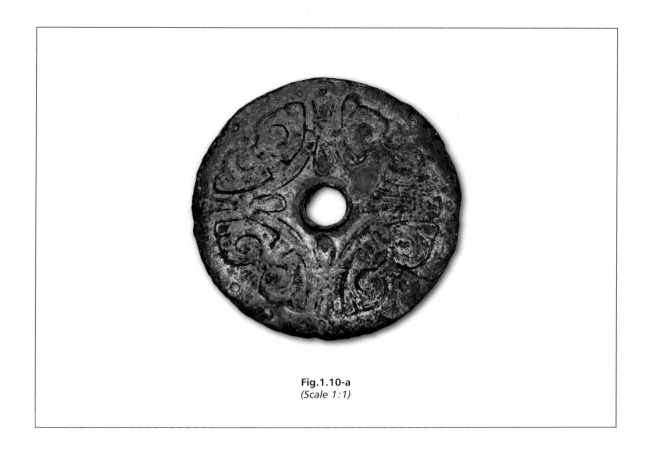

Fig.1.10-a
(Scale 1:1)

1.10 ECCLESIASTICAL & LITURGICAL ITEMS

The Late Anglo-Saxon church was provided with a great deal of wealth, enabling it to commission works of art for the greater glory of God. There is evidence for bell-casting from Gloucester and Winchester in the late 10th and 11th centuries, although no actual bells are known to have survived.

Fig.1.10-a. A Late Saxon or Hiberno-Norse reliquary mount, comprising a thick silver facing plate on a copper-alloy backing. The layout of the disc's surface decoration is similar to the Winchester Style double-contoured rounded lozenges found on the Anglo-Scandinavian Sutton (Isle of Eley) brooch. The motifs consist of fleshy acanthus-leaf ornaments which spring from a truncated stump in involuted scrolls similar to those seen on the *Winchester Psalter* and other mid-11th century Anglo-Saxon manuscripts. The mount has some yellow/ochre enamelling and eight small perforations equally spaced around the rim to facilitate fixing. The findspot is unknown.

Fig.1.10-b
(Scale 2.5:1)

Fig.1.10-b. A 12th century high-status mount in the form of a rectangular gold plate, with edge strips soldered on to form a shallow 'tray', with a 'fleur de lis' outlined in beaded wire, secured to that backplate with small wire clasps and with a few applied granules. The form suggests that this is an inlay mount; perhaps once set into a book cover or similar. It is from an old European collection, findspot unknown.

89

Fig.1.10-c
(Scale 1.5:1)

Fig.1.10-d
(Scale 1:1)

Fig.1.10-c. A beautiful 10th century silver cross consisting of a large central disc with four arms branching out each terminating with a spherical finial; the lower arm is slightly longer than the others. The central field is inscribed with 'AG' on one side and 'LA' on the other, in neat seriffed Roman capitals. The large, cast suspension loop is attached to the top of the upper finial. Findspot unknown.

Fig.1.10-d. A 12th century Anglo-Norman gilt-bronze Limoges mount cast gilt-bronze T-shaped plate with decoration reserved against a plain field for champ-levé enamel; the design is based on an eagle with raised wings, probably forming one arm of a decorated altar or processional cross. It has four holes to accept attachment rivets. It was found in Suffolk.

Fig.1.10-e
(Scale 1:1)

Fig.1.10-e. A complete set of cast bronze Limoges work plaques for a devotional cross. The four T-shaped plaques were designed to be fixed to an altar cross, each provided with four fixing holes, their surfaces bearing figural decoration in champ-levé technique (the enamel no longer present). A fifth plaque is rectangular with two fixing holes, with the letters IHS in champ-levé. Some gilding remains on the decorative surfaces. Findspot unknown.

Fig.1.10-h
(Scale 1:1)

Fig.1.10-h. A 12th century lead seal from a document issued by Pope Lucius III. It was found in Essex.

Fig.1.10-f
(Scale 1.25:1)

Fig.1.10-f. A cast copper-alloy openwork book mount with attachment hole in the chest, the legs in openwork. The attitude of the beast is reminiscent of the 'howling wolf' seen on contemporary 11th century stirrup mounts. From the Kennis collection.

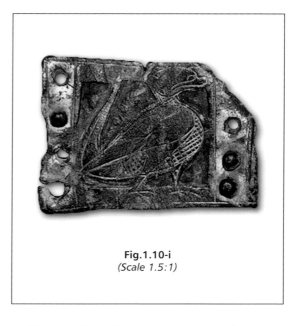

Fig.1.10-i
(Scale 1.5:1)

Fig.1.10-g
(Scale 1:1)

Fig.1.10-g. A 12th century 'papal bulla', a lead seal from a document issued by Pope Alexander III. The iconography of papal bulls has not altered since the time of Pope Pasquale II (1099-1118) - one face bears the name of the issuing Pope and the other the opposed profile heads of SS. Peter and Paul with a cruciform emblem between and a form of the identifying abbreviated legend 'SPASPE', (Sanctus Paulus Sanctus Petrus 'Saint Paul, Saint Peter') on the other. The present example features the legend ALEX/ANDER/PP.III. It was found near Norwich, Norfolk.

Fig.1.10-i. A 12th century copper-alloy plate or mount with polychrome champ-levé design between two gilt borders each pierced with four rivet holes (three rivets remaining). The design comprises a stylised dark blue bird facing right on a turquoise enamelled background, its neck and chest executed in incised hatched blocks. The bird image is a good example of Romanesque Style which came to England in the reign of Edward the Confessor but only became popular in the following century. By the early 12th century, goldsmiths at the Benedictine abbey of Conques were able to produce enamelled panels with vivid colours and golden surfaces. The enamels made in the French city of Limoges became an artistic hallmark of the region. It was found in Nottinghamshire.

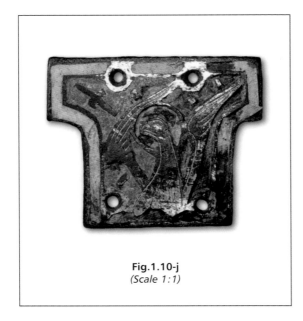

Fig.1.10-j
(Scale 1:1)

Fig.1.10-j. A 12th-13th century T-shaped Limoges work plaque pierced in four places for attachment to a large cross, reliquary or other object of veneration. The design comprises a white enamel border enclosing a pale blue enamelled panel containing the nimbate winged lion of St. Mark with most of its gilding remaining. A cross and elements of a foliate design are placed around the lion. The champlevé technique is carefully managed to produce feathering on the wings. It was found in Cambridgeshire.

Fig.1.10-k
(Scale 1:1)

Fig.1.10-k. A copper-alloy cast figure of Christ crucified from the 11th-12th century, wearing a three-lobed crown, the ribs and loincloth delineated with engraved lines; the facial features modelled in the round, engraved and enhanced; with affixing holes to hands and at feet (two rivets remaining) with traces of gilding. The figurine is executed in Romanesque style, similar to examples in the collection of Cambridge University Museum of Archaeology and Anthropology. It was found at Norwich, Norfolk in 1981.

Fig.1.10-l. A finely made and colourful enamelled Limoges mount depicting a churchman in his mantle with arms protruding at the front. The eyes are silvered for effect. From the Kennis collection.

Fig.1.10-m. A 12th century cast bronze tongue-shaped Limoges mount with human head above modelled in the round, and enamelled cellwork to the flat body. It is pierced in two places for attachment. It was found at Alderton, Suffolk.

Fig.1.10-l
(Scale 1:1)

Fig.1.10-m
(Scale 1:1)

Fig.1.10-n. A cast gilt-bronze Limoges mount of 12th century date with tongue-shaped body and head; the body with panels of white enamel and two circular piercings; the neck slender and head D-shaped with fine facial features and black glass bead eyes. It was found in Continental Europe.

Fig.1.10-o. A 12th century D-shaped mount pierced in two places for attachment to a cross, reliquary or other object of veneration. The surface of the mount is silvered and a radiating geometric design is added in champ-levé with dark blue-green enamel. On the upper edge is a human head modelled in the round with enamel points for the eyes. The face is tilted upwards and the rest of the mount forms a cloak or chasuble. This class of object is associated particularly with the Abbey of Grandmont at Limoges under the patronage of Henri II (fl. AD 1133-1189). It was found in County Durham.

Fig.1.10-p
(Scale 1.25:1)

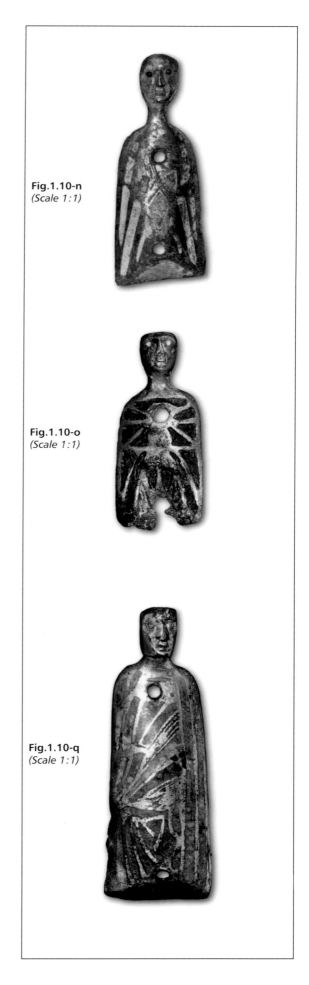

Fig.1.10-n
(Scale 1:1)

Fig.1.10-o
(Scale 1:1)

Fig.1.10-q
(Scale 1:1)

Fig.1.10-p. A hollow-cast mount in the form of a human male in classical robes with hands folded across the upper chest. The lower body is absent and the torso is twisted to one side, probably to join onto another fitting. The eyes are almond-shaped, the nose and cheeks bulbous, the folds of cloth indicated by raised ribs. A small hole in the neck accepted the attachment pin. It was found in East Anglia.

Fig.1.10-q. A cast gilt-bronze 12th century Limoges mount, D-shaped and hollow to the reverse, formed with a human face above, modelled in the round. The body is decorated with radiating panels in green enamel and two vertical bands to the right side. It is pierced in two places for attachment. From an European collection.

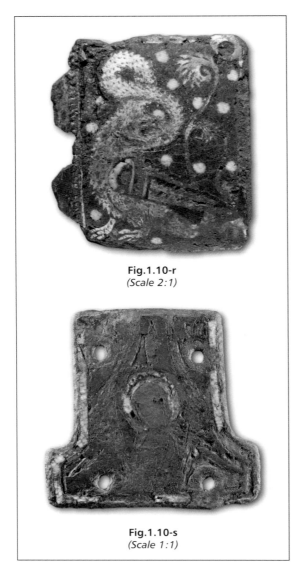

Fig.1.10-r
(Scale 2:1)

Fig.1.10-s
(Scale 1:1)

Fig.1.11-a
(Scale 2:1)

Fig.1.10-r. A beautifully enamelled Limoges mount with a Romanesque style bird on a pelletted field. The surviving enamel colours demonstrate how vibrant such artefacts were when new. From the Kennis collection.

Fig.1.10-s. A cast copper-alloy T-shaped mount with four attachment holes. The mount retains much of the blue and white enamel fill for the champ-levé panels which form the design of a nimbate figure in a robe within a border. The plate formed the decorative panel for the lower arm of an ecclesiastical cross. It was found at Sutton-on-the-Hill, Derbyshire.

1.11 GAMING PIECES

Gaming of various kinds was a popular pastime in Anglo-Scandinavian England, both games of chance using dice on a board and more tactical games such as 'Fox and Geese'. Chess reached Europe from the Near East around AD 1000, and displaced older tactical games, such as *hnefatafl*, as the preferred amusement of the élite.

Fig.1.11-a. A cast bronze figurine depicting a horse and rider with kite-shaped shield and conical helmet, carefully modelled reins and surcoat; there is no indication of a sword or spear in the rider's hand. The shape of the shield and helmet indicate a probable 12th century date, as well as the full covering for the horse which would develop into the later medieval heraldic caparison. The rider's face is clearly defined with neat moustache and beard. The folds of the cloth surcoat and saddle-blanket are executed naturalistically in the Romanesque Style. There is some evidence of silvering or tinning of the surface, which would be necessary if both sets of gaming pieces were cast in the same metal from the same moulds; one set could be silvered, tinned, gilded, painted or enamelled to disinguish them from their untreated bronze opponents. There is evidence of solder to the underside, perhaps indicating that it was fixed to a separately-made base.

Gaming pieces were a high-status accessory for elite males in the medieval period, as seen also in the carved examples from the Isle of Lewis (2.4.2-a) and later cast examples, some even made in pipeclay; there may have been wooden examples which do not survive.

Warriors, noblemen and military leaders used boardgames to encourage the tactical thinking and strategic awareness which served them in warfare. The gaming piece was found in Nottinghamshire and is now in the Nottingham Castle Museum.

1.12 WEIGHTS & TRADE ITEMS

Trade weights were produced in some quantity in Byzantium during the Later Saxon period and reached England either via Francia or in the pouches of Scandinavian merchants. Seal matrices and lead seals began to be used in England in the Norman period, and quickly became a common item of use among merchants.

Fig.1.12-a. A polyhedral weight of magnificent workmanship, with inset garnet cloisons to the upper face and a gold annulet to the top. The style is reminiscent of the garnet-and-gold jewellery of the 7th century and it is possible that it was converted from the head of a dress pin.

Fig.1.12-b. A 10th-11th century weight of Scandinavian 'barrel' profile, formed as a copper-alloy casing around a denser iron core. On the upper face is a design of a hooked cross with annulet ends within two concentric pelletted bands; a similar design is on the lower face and there are punched-point triangles and radiating star designs on the sides. The weight is equivalent to four of the standard Norse ortug weights of 8.22 grams. It was found in Norfolk.

Fig.1.12-c. This Late Viking (11th century AD) rounded conical trade weight, cast in copper-alloy, has a trefoil extension at the top with the upper lobe cut square. Its sides are decorated with punched roundel motifs in vertical bands. The base features a small central indentation. It was found in Cambridgeshire.

Fig.1.12-d. An Anglo-Saxon or Viking conical lead weight with embedded copper-alloy stud, with serrated outer edge and incised cross patty in the domed centre. It dates from the 8th-11th century. It was found in York, Yorkshire.

Fig.1.12-e. A gold ingot of rectangular section with recesses to the broader faces, possibly Viking. The ingot tapers towards one end and the shorter sides are facetted. Unknown findspot.

Fig.1.12-f. A Viking or Anglo-Scandinavian D-section ingot or cast bar with rounded ends, slightly splayed on one face. The metal is an alloy of lead and copper, and the silvery metallic surface is visible beneath the cuprous patination. It was found at Stamford Bridge, Yorkshire.

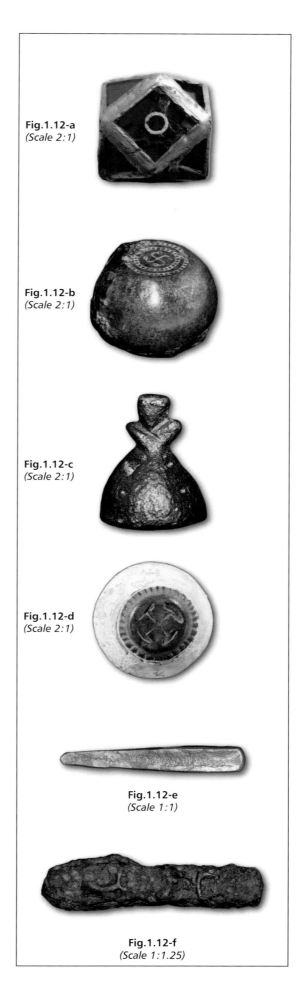

Fig.1.12-a
(Scale 2:1)

Fig.1.12-b
(Scale 2:1)

Fig.1.12-c
(Scale 2:1)

Fig.1.12-d
(Scale 2:1)

Fig.1.12-e
(Scale 1:1)

Fig.1.12-f
(Scale 1:1.25)

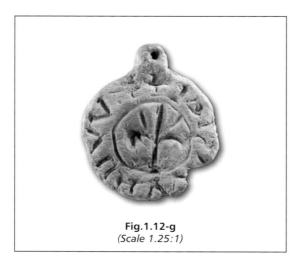

Fig.1.12-g
(Scale 1.25:1)

Fig.1.12-g. An Anglo-Norman flat disc personal seal matrix pendant with pierced lobe suspension mount. The central roundel bears a fleur-de-lys; around this is the legend +VVIL […], presumably a personal name such as William. It was found in Tilbury, Essex.

1.13 HOUSEHOLD OBJECTS

Domestic items, although numerous, are not a common find in English soil: many were made from low-grade metal and have become unrecognisable in the intervening centuries. There are, nevertheless, some astonishing examples of items of everyday use from the 11th and 12th centuries.

Fig.1.13-a
(Scale 1:1.25)

Fig.1.13-a. A 12th century bronze candle holder in the form of dog with erect head and neck, recurved tail and hatched panels to flanks; the spike attached to the shoulders. The workmanship is Norman Sicilian. From the Netherlands.

Fig.1.13-b
(Scale 1:1)

Fig.1.13-b. A cast bronze figure of a standing dog, with curled tail and elliptical eyes, hatched texture to the flanks and legs. It dates from the 11th-12th century AD and was found in Somerset.

Fig.1.13-c
(Scale 1.5:1)

Fig.1.13-c. A characteristic 10th-12th century eastern Baltic silver barrel-shaped spacer bead of Viking design, from a decorative necklace. The barrel-shaped tube is decorated with four equidistant bands of thick silver filigree; between the outer bands are a series of filigree hoops. It is of Scandinavian origin.

Fig.1.13-d
(Scale 1.25:1)

Fig.1.13-d. An openwork cast 'looped' handle in copper-alloy for a firesteel in the form of a long, triangular serpentine head with punched-dot eyes and nostrils, and extended tongue in the 11th century Anglo-Scandinavian style. The reverse edge of the firesteel is decorated with three parallel incised lines. There is ferrous incrustation from the steel striking plate on the lateral surfaces. It was found in East Anglia.

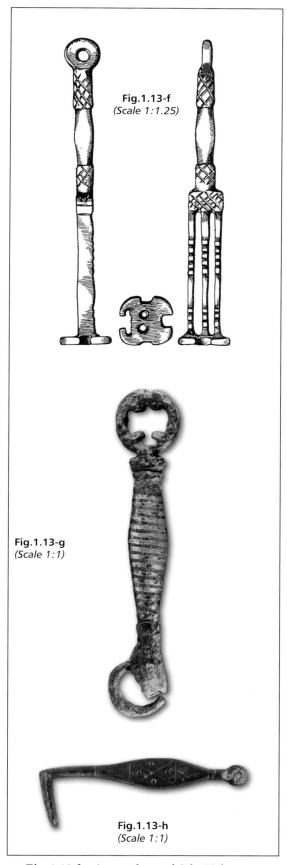

Fig.1.13-f
(Scale 1:1.25)

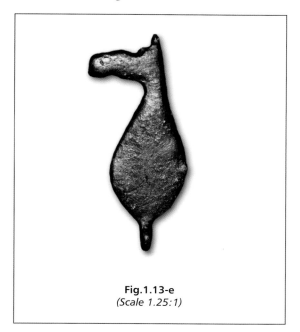

Fig.1.13-e
(Scale 1.25:1)

Fig.1.13-e. An 11th century key. Rotating latch keys were introduced towards the end of the Anglo-Saxon period, replacing latch-lifters and other security devices based on displacing the internal springs of a padlock. Most of these items were probably used on chests and cupboards rather than house-doors at this time. The body of the key is a solid elliptical casting similar to a number of pierced examples from the later Anglo-Saxon period. There is a cast suspension loop at the lower end. The plain shank is shaped to accommodate the internal mechanism of the lock. It was found in Nottinghamshire

Fig.1.13-f. A Scandinavian cast copper-alloy padlock key with suspension loop, barrelled shaft and three bars supporting the transverse plate: the recesses and holes in the plate form the wards of the key. It was found in Denmark.

Fig.1.13-g. A cast bronze 10th-11th century key comprising a biconical shaft with loop and suspension ring at one end, openwork disc at the other, with openwork cruciform centre; the shaft with a spiral of gilded inlay. Ex Barker collection; found on the Thames foreshore at Billingsgate.

Fig.1.13-g
(Scale 1:1)

Fig.1.13-h
(Scale 1:1)

Fig.1.13-h. A cast key of 8th-10th century date, comprising an elliptical plate, small bow and right-angled ward; the plate is decorated to both faces with an incised saltire and four dots. It was found in Nottinghamshire.

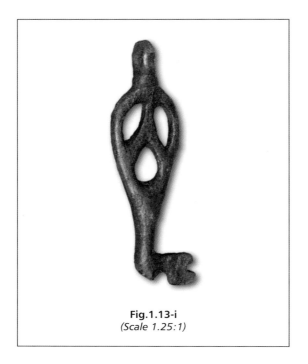

Fig.1.13-i
(Scale 1.25:1)

Fig.1.13-j
(Scale 1:1)

Fig.1.13-i. A cast bronze casket key with transverse suspension loop, openwork elliptical bow and toothing on the lower edge of the bit. It dates from the 9th-11th century and was found at Catterick, Yorkshire.

Fig.1.13-j. An 11th-12th century bronze barrel key with single right-angled ward, one tooth to short and one to long edge, solid ovoid bow, suspension loop attached. It was found in Yorkshire.

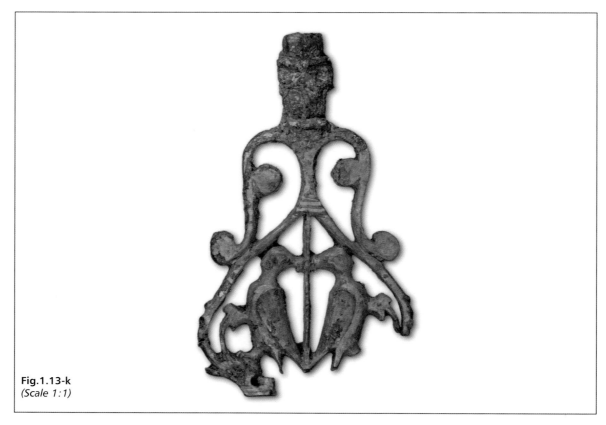

Fig.1.13-k
(Scale 1:1)

Fig.1.13-k. An 11th-12th century cast bronze openwork handle formed as a pair of opposed birds within a floral frame, with hinge above. The style of the metalwork is influenced by the European Romanesque but may show some contemporary North African influence; it was probably made in Sicily.

Fig.1.13-l
(Scale 1.25:1)

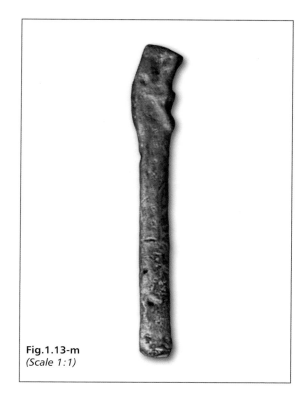

Fig.1.13-m
(Scale 1:1)

Fig.1.13-l. An 11th-12th century AD cast gilt-bronze lock-plate with a slot and two round holes, with a spigot to the reverse. At the top is a frontal beast-head with lentoid eyes and notched fringe. It was found in Cambridgeshire.

Fig.1.13-m. A long knife or tool handle, with the end moulded in the shape of a snake's or dragon's head, while the distal end consists of a V-shaped notch filled with the remains of the iron blade. The head and body are covered with ring and dot decoration. A 10th century date has been suggested for this item. It was found in Norfolk.

Fig.1.13-n. An 11th-12th century Norman ribbed swivel terminal, probably from a hunting dog's lead. The profile of the swivel appears to show a highly stylised pair of canine heads. It was found in Hampshire.

Fig.1.13-o. A pair of 11th-12th century cast copper-alloy swivel-mount rings, each loop formed as a pair of opposed zoomorphic heads. The swivel is created from two hemispherical sections, one with a pin and the other pierced. The pin is inserted through the piercing and flattened over to trap it. There are transverse bands on the lower parts of the swivel halves. The piece is complete and still articulated. These mounts were used to strengthen the point where a leather strap had to turn freely through a wide arc. It was found in Lincolnshire.

Fig.1.13-n
(Scale 1.5:1)

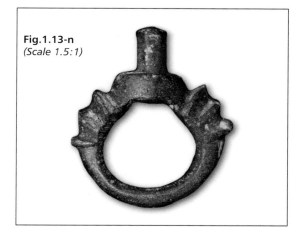

Fig.1.13-o
(Scale 1.5:1)

Fig.1.13-p
(Scale 1.25:1)

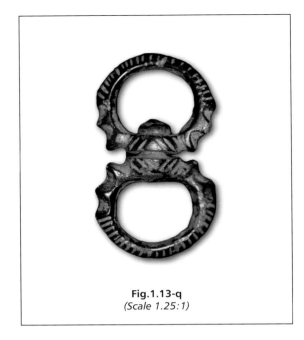

Fig.1.13-q
(Scale 1.25:1)

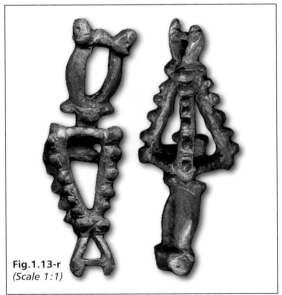

Fig.1.13-r
(Scale 1:1)

Fig.1.13-s
(Scale 1.25:1)

Fig.1.13-p. A pair of cast, copper-alloy swivel-mount rings, segmented with transverse banding which extends on to the swivel halves. The swivel is created from two hemispherical sections, one with a pin and the other pierced. It was found in Lincolnshire and dates from the 11th-12th century.

Fig.1.13-q. A pair of 11th-12th century cast swivel-mount rings, each loop formed as a pair of opposed zoomorphic heads clutching the swivel-half in its jaws. The attachment tags are still in place, which were riveted in three places to the leather straps. It was found in Lincolnshire.

Fig.1.13-r. An unusual 11th-12th century swivel, the body of which seems to have been carved from a pyramidal cast block with a V-shaped strap attachment 'loop' extending from the apex, in the form of two extended conjoined snake heads. The open-work body is decorated with globular knobs along the edges and larger globules extending from the corners. The swivel section has a long spigot with a larger similar elongated strap attachment made up of two conjoined dogs with arched backs facing each other, joined at the hind legs and again under the chin. It was found on a Norman 'skirmish' site at Fen Drayton, Huntingdonshire.

Fig.1.13-s. A pair of cast bronze 11th-12th century swivel-mount rings, each loop formed as a pair of opposed zoomorphic heads clutching the swivel-half in its jaws. The swivel was probably developed to prevent tangling in the leashes of hunting dogs. It was found in Norfolk.

Anglo-Saxon Earldoms in AD 1045

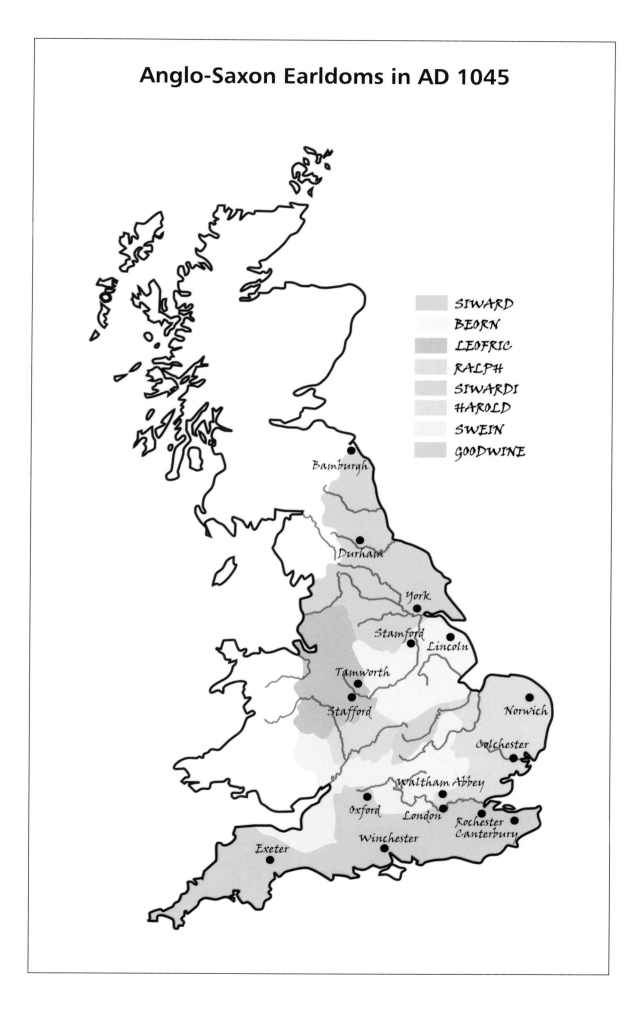

SIWARD
BEORN
LEOFRIC
RALPH
SIWARDI
HAROLD
SWEIN
GOODWINE

Bamburgh

Durham

York

Stamford
Lincoln

Tamworth

Stafford

Norwich

Colchester

Waltham Abbey

Oxford
London
Rochester
Canterbury

Winchester

Exeter

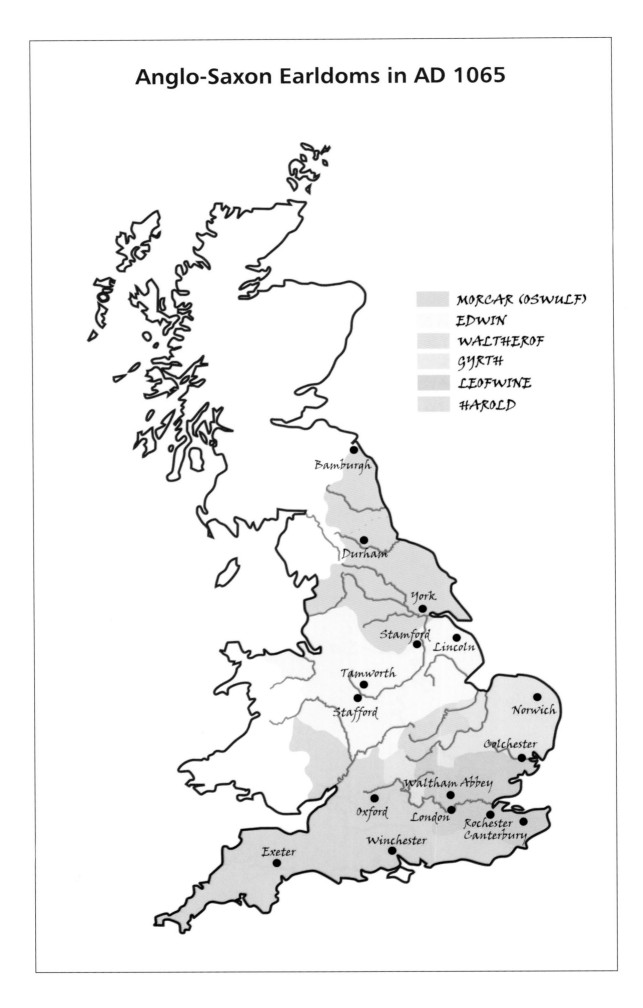

Anglo-Saxon Earldoms in AD 1065

MORCAR (OSWULF)
EDWIN
WALTHEROF
GYRTH
LEOFWINE
HAROLD

Bamburgh

Durham

York

Stamford

Lincoln

Tamworth

Stafford

Norwich

Colchester

Waltham Abbey

Oxford

London

Rochester
Canterbury

Winchester

Exeter

2. Non-Metallic Artefacts

2.1 TEXTILES

The most famous early medieval textile remains must be the Bayeux tapestry, which hangs around the walls of the church of Bayeux, France. At over 70 metres long and half a metre wide, the 'tapestry' – really an embroidery since the design is formed with additional threads, not woven into the fabric – was produced in sections by women working from both the top and the bottom of the frame.

The version of events is told from the Norman point of view, as would be expected in a work commissioned by a Norman clergyman, but the narrative is at pains to show Harold Godwineson as a noble warrior and statesman and his army as fierce and formidable. (There would be little glory attached to William's victory if the English opponents were described as weak and cowardly.) The embroidery is executed in Romanesque style,

It was probably made in England (perhaps at Winchester or Canterbury) by a team of skilled women over a period of some months. The 'tapestry' shows in some detail the events of 1066 from the death of Edward the Confessor through to the coronation of William I; the visual record is made up from many scenes like a cartoon strip, accompanied by a terse narrative in Latin. Interestingly, the upper and lower borders often show little vignettes of 11th century life, such as men fowling with a sling and stones, or looters on a battlefield stripping the fallen warriors of their armour.

and is the best surviving example of *Opus Anglicanum* "English Work", a much-prized form of textile in the 11th century AD.

The details of arms and armour, tableware and clothing are very helpful in assessing the material culture of Late Anglo-Saxon England and the early Norman period. The warriors' shields are mostly of the 'tear-drop' pattern but some English warriors use round shields and large axes.

The most famous scene shows a warrior with an arrow in his eye, under the words

'Harold Rex' (King Harold), leading to the belief that Harold was accidentally killed by a stray arrow. A reproduction of the design from 1729 does not show the arrow, suggesting that the fabric may have been repaired (there are several places where this has been attempted) and the arrow added at that time. The words 'Harold Rex' are followed by 'interfectus est' (is slain) and it may be that the figure of the king is the recumbent body further on in the scene.

2.2 STONE

Norman arch in a doorway at South Cerney church

The Normans are predominantly associated with the widespread erection of stone buildings in England, using the Romanesque style with blind arcading and round-headed arches decorated with geometric patterns. It is very likely (but has never been proven) that Edward the Confessor and his Norman favourites may have introduced Romanesque architecture to England in the mid-11th century, thus pushing the earliest use of the 'Norman' style back by several decades. It is probable that the first Westminster Abbey, commissioned by Edward, was a Romanesque building. Romanesque architecture was not a Norman innovation, but was copied from the contemporary Frankish culture.

2.2.1 Sculpture

Late Anglo-Saxon England enjoyed a rich tradition of sculpture, much of it sadly damaged by the Normans and at the Reformation. Some examples of religious sculpture, such as the famous panel in Sompting church with its Anglo-Saxon and Romanesque features, can be compared with pure Scandinavian pieces such as the tombstone from St. Pauls, London.

Fig.2.2.1-a
(Not to scale)

Fig.2.2.1-a. Runestone from St. Paul's London.

The stone, which dates from about AD 1000, bears a Scandinavian runic text along its edges, among the last known uses of the runic script in England.

The stone was erected in the churchyard of St. Paul's and is decorated with a high-relief Ringerike Style designs comprising a large regardant beast with a smaller one enmeshed in its forelegs, possibly derived from the classic 'hare and hound' motif used since Roman times. The bilinear text commemorates the two Scandinavians who set it up, named Ginna and Toki. The surface of the stone was originally painted: the field was white, the beasts black and the frame, tendrils and limbs ochre.

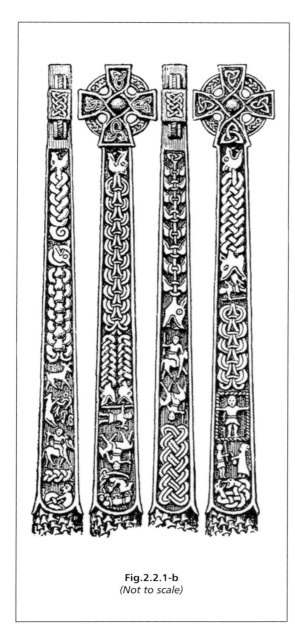

Fig.2.2.1-b
(Not to scale)

Fig.2.2.1-b. The Gosforth Cross, Cumbria. The Gosforth Cross is a large stone Anglo-Scandinavian cross in the churchyard of St Mary's, Gosforth, Cumbria; it dates from the 10th century. The cross is carved with scenes from Norse mythology, including the trickster god Loki bound to a rock; the god *Heimdallr* holding his horn which will be blown at the final battle in which the gods are destroyed; *Oðinn's* son *Viðarr* tearing open the jaws of the wolf Fenrir; Thor's trying to catch *Jörmungandr*, the Great Serpent.

2.2.2 Quernstones

Rotary querns continued in use in the Anglo-Scandinavian period, and evidence from areas such as Southampton suggests that they did not differ in the 12th century from their earlier forms.

2.2.3 Whetstones

Portable whetstones, in the form of stone bars around 7cm long and drilled at one end, remained in use throughout the period. Scriptoria used small knives for sharpening their quills frequently, and whetstones are a common find on such sites.

2.2.4 Finger Rings

Finger rings made from minerals such as agate were known in the Middle and Late Saxon periods.

2.2.5 Amber Beads

Fig.2.2.5-a
(Scale 1:1)

Fig.2.2.5-a. A mixed group of large graduated amber beads; barrel-shaped, discoid and plano-convex in profile. They are from a London collection, 9th-11th century in date.

2.3 GLASS

Glass working in England was a small-scale industry, because glass was a premium product which could not be afforded by most people. However, small items such as beads and rings were produced in some quantity. It is likely that most Anglo-Scandinavian glass objects were recycled from broken or obsolete items as cullet.

2.3.1 Beads

Glass beads do not feature in the archaeology of Anglo-Scandinavian England, although they continue to be found in Denmark and it is therefore á priori likely that many females continued to use them as symbols of wealth.

2.3.2 Window Glass

Window glass was known in England from the 7th century onwards, although very little survives due to the re-use of broken glass to create new objects. Painted fragments sometimes bear decoration in the Winchester Style, suggesting an 11th century date.

2.3.3 Glass Vessels

Glass vessels from the Anglo-Scandinavian period are not common, but it is notable that the Bayeux Tapestry (see 2.1) shows a man drinking from a shallow palm-cup, similar to several examples excavated from 7th century tombs (i.e. Loveden Hill, Lincolnshire) suggesting that traditional forms of tableware were not entirely obsolete at the period of the Norman invasion.

2.3.4 Finger Rings

There is some evidence for glass finger rings from the Late Saxon period, made by shaping a blob of molten glass around a metal rod.

2.4 BONE & IVORY

Bone was used for a variety of purposes, notably knife handles and small domestic items.

2.4.1 Bone & Ivory Tools

Many household items were always produced in bone, into early modern times. These include needles, combs, small containers and spoons. The carving of figural scenes in ivory seems to have become a standard form of late Saxon ornament, and several fine pieces are known, mostly with religious connections.

Fig.2.4.1-a
(Scale 1:1)

Fig.2.4.1-a. A seal matrix of 11th century date found at Wallingford, carved from ivory, features a man's emblem on one side (*Godwini ministri* 'of Godwin the thane') and on the other a female version (*Godgyðe monache dodate* 'of Godgyð, a nun given to God').

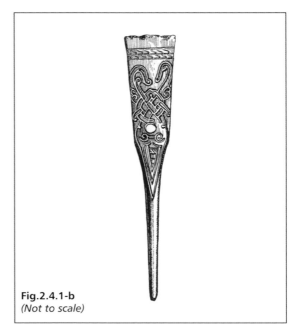

Fig.2.4.1-b
(Not to scale)

Fig.2.4.1-b. A bone pin used to fasten a cloak – a lace or thong on the edge of the cloak was passed through the hole in the pin, then wound round the shaft. The pin is decorated with Ringerike Style carving, and has been polished by long use. The bone came from a pig. Found in the River Thames.

Fig.2.4.1-c
(Scale 1:1)

Fig.2.4.2-a
(Not to scale)

Fig.2.4.1-c. An 11th century D-shaped multipart bone comb comprising two thin plates with sawn teeth, two D-shaped outer plates with ring-and-dot design, and three securing rivets.

2.4.2 Bone & Ivory Gaming Pieces

The 'Lewis Chessmen' is the name given to a set of ornamented gaming pieces, found on the Isle of Lewis, Scotland in AD 1831. The group comprises 78 individual pieces, carved in walrus ivory or whale's tooth, and dating to the 12th century based on the clothing, weapons and armour depicted. They are probably of Norwegian manufacture, perhaps in the port of Trondheim: Lewis, as part of the Outer Hebrides, was under Norse domination at this time. Aside from the chessmen, some plain gaming counters or discs were found, and an ivory belt buckle. The group has been interpreted as the stock of a carver or dealer in ivory goods. The circumstances of discovery are disputed, but most accounts agree that they came from a cist or stone-lined grave: whether they were buried with their owner, or hidden by him with the intention of recovering them, will never be known.

Most of the pieces are carved as humans: armoured horsemen, sword-wielding footsoldiers, bishops with crosiers, kings and queens seated in their thrones. The pawns are carved as rounded posts with geometric detailing.

Fig.2.4.2-a. A king sitting with his sword on his knees, his hair falling in four strands behind; a queen in a robe with a mantle over the top and a headrail beneath her crown.

2.5 HORN

Horn was a valuable and versatile material which was used for a variety of purposes in Anglo-Saxon and Norman times. It does not survive well archaeologically so most horn products are probably unrecorded.

2.5.1 Drinking Horns

Drinking horns continued in use into the Anglo-Scandinavian period: although no finds have been recognised, the Bayeux tapestry (below) shows men seated, drinking from horns.

Detail from the Bayeux tapestry: King Harold and his men dine in his residence at Bosham, Sussex. Two have drinking horns, while the central figure, Harold, has a palm-cup

2.5.2 Ink horns

A Late Saxon period artefact is the *blæcærn* or ink horn, referred to in one of the *Exeter Book* riddles. None has ever been identified, but since they may have had no metal fittings there may not be any physical remains to study. Manuscript production in the Late Saxon and Norman periods relied on the services of trained scribes, not all of whom need have been ecclesiastics.

2.5.3 Lanterns

Horn lanterns were devised by King Alfred in the 9th century as a means of protecting candles from draughts. Since Alfred also devised a means of measuring time using candles, it seems likely that lanterns with horn plates in the sides were in use houses and religious establishments in the Late Saxon period. The accurate measurement of time was important in religious communities where services were supposed to take place at set times during the day and night.

2.5.4 Blast Horns

A blast or blowing horn was used to signal the presence of travellers on the road, according to one law-code. Horns are also shown in manuscript illustrations being blown by huntsmen and warriors.

2.6. CERAMIC

Ceramics played an increasingly important role in the domestic environment during the Late Saxon period, perhaps indicating that access to pottery vessels was becoming more widespread geographically and socially. Individual vessel types have been identified, as well as specific pottery fabrics; by plotting the distribution of these, it is possible to plot trade routes and economic regions.

2.6.1 Vessels

The pottery industry seems to have made great advances in the Later Saxon period, with several new types of fabric and vessel coming onto the market. Most Anglo-Saxon and Anglo-Norman pottery is referenced by the fabric or 'ware', in several specific types:

Chester ware – 10th-11th century - a hard, sandy brown ware, wheel-thrown and kiln-fired, found in the region of Chester and western Mercia. The pots have a flanged rim, rouletted shoulder and rounded base.

Fine Whitby ware – a grey or black ware found only on monastic sites in the north of England. It is wheel-thrown and kiln-fired, and the only vessel type is a squat pot with an everted rim.

Leicester ware - 10th-11th century – sandy grey ware with quartz inclusions, wheel-thrown and kiln-fired, found in the Leicester area. It is used for pots and storage jars.

Lincoln ware – a hard, sandy ware, dark grey to russet in colour, with a silky finish due to being fired at a high temperature. It is used for bulbous cooking pots and bowls with rouletting decoration. It is confined to the Lincoln area.

Michelmersh ware - 10th-11th century – a smooth brown ware, wheel-thrown and kiln-fired. It is used for a variety of purposes, including spouted jugs, cooking pots and tableware (dishes, etc.).

Northampton ware – a hard, sandy ware, grey to brown in colour, only found in Northampton. It is used mainly for cooking pots.

Porchester ware - 10th-11th century – a hard russet to brown ware, wheel-thrown and kiln-fired, tempered with crushed flint, only found in the Porchester area. It is used for dishes and bowls, and for squat cooking pots.

St. Neots ware – a soft ware, black, grey or russet in colour, tempered with crushed shell. It was wheel-thrown but fired to a low temperature in a clamp. It was used for cooking pots and lamps, but is most associated with 'spouted' bowls, storage jars; it is found in the east Midlands from Cambridgeshire to Durham.

Stamford ware – 9th-12th century – a white or pink ware which occurs in two forms: a fine, glazed type used for spouted pitchers and tableware, and coarse form used for cooking pots. The glazed surface can be green, yellow or orange in colour. It was thrown on a fast wheel, and often decorated with rouletting and applied strips. It is found almost everywhere in England by the 10th century, and as far afield as Dublin.

Thetford ware – a hard, grey ware, wheel-thrown and kiln-fired, tempered with sand. Production centres have been identified at Thetford, Ipswich and Norwich. It is used for cooking pots and jars, some very large, often with stamped designs.

Torksey ware– 10th-12th century - similar to Thetford ware but rougher in texture due to quartz inclusions.

Winchester ware – 10th-11th century – a wheel-thrown, sandy brown ware with a lead-based glaze varying from pale russet to dark green in colour. It is often decorated with stamps, applied strips and rouletting and is found across southern England, with a concentration in the Winchester area. It is used for cups, bowls, pots, jars, pitchers and imitation costrels (ceramic vessels decorated to look like leatherware).

York ware – 10th-12th century – a gritty, hard ware fired at a high temperature, used for jars and cooking pots.

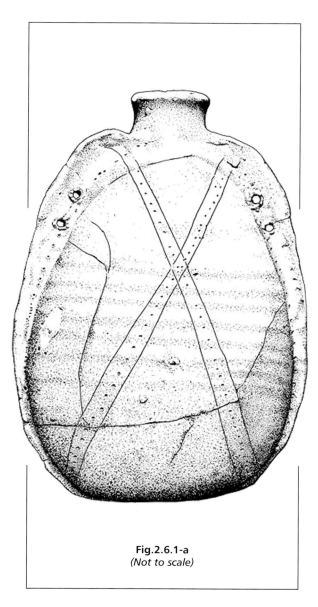

Fig.2.6.1-a
(Not to scale)

Fig.2.6.1-a. A Winchester ware ceramic costrel with piercings to the border and imitation leather straps to the sides.

2.6.2 Spindle Whorls & Loom Weights

Loom weights continued to be made from ceramic in the Late Saxon period as they had been since the Iron Age. They were doughnut-shaped and generally unornamented. Spindle whorls were probably also made in ceramic at this time. Both items were essential for the production of wool and woollen textiles, which was the foundation of the rural economy in some areas. Viking textile technology was not greatly different from Anglo-Saxon, although there are some techniques for knitting and weaving very warm textiles which seem to be confined to Scandinavia.

2.6.3 Floor Tiles

Glazed ceramic floor tiles were found in the Late Saxon levels of Winchester, decorated in geometric, tessellated patterns.

Fig.2.6.3-a
(Not to scale)

Fig.2.6.3-a. A geometric-patterned ceramic floor tile from Winchester, 10th-11th century AD.

2.7 WOOD

Wood was the foundation of the English economy, along with wool, through to the early modern period. Wood was used for buildings (even stone buildings were erected with wooden scaffolding), for ships, for waggons, for tools and for fuel to make all the output of ovens, smithies and kilns which made life possible.

Anglo-Saxon Towns with Mints AD 957-1016

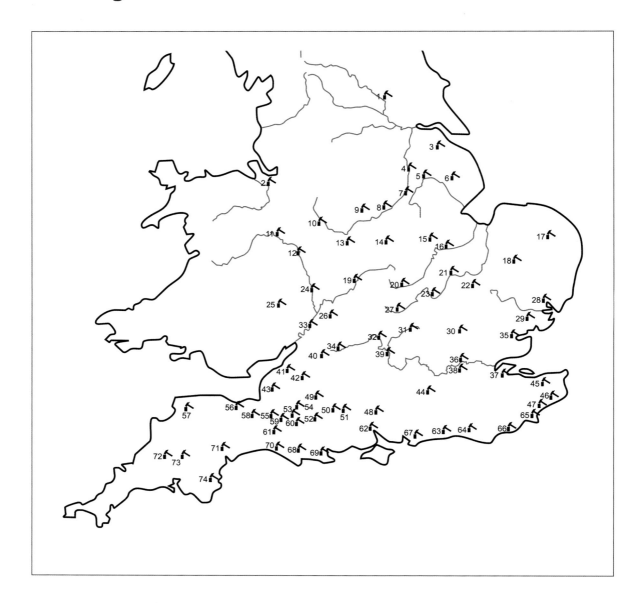

1 York	21 Huntingdon	41 Bristol	61 Crewkerne
2 Chester	22 Cambridge	42 Bath	62 Southampton
3 Caistor	23 Bedford	43 Axbridge	63 Cissbury
4 Torksey	24 Worcester	44 Guildford	64 Lewes
5 Lincoln	25 Hereford	45 Canterbury	65 Romney
6 Horncastle	26 Winchcombe	46 Dover	66 Hastings
7 Newark	27 Buckingham	47 Lympne	67 Chichester
8 Nottingham	28 Ipswich	48 Winchester	68 Dorchester
9 Derby	29 Colchester	49 Warminster	69 Wareham
10 Stafford	30 Hertford	50 Wilton	70 Bridport
11 Shrewsbury	31 Aylesbury	51 Salisbury	71 Exeter
12 Bridgnorth	32 Oxford	52 Shaftesbury	72 Launceston
13 Tamworth	33 Gloucester	53 Cadbury	73 Lydford
14 Leicester	34 Cricklade	54 Bruton	74 Totnes
15 Stamford	35 Maldon	55 Langport	
16 Peterborough	36 London	56 Watchet	
17 Norwich	37 Rochester	57 Barnstaple	
18 Thetford	38 Southwark	58 Taunton	
19 Warwick	39 Wallingford	59 Ilchester	
20 Northampton	40 Malmesbury	60 Milbourne	

3. Manufacturing Techniques

The techniques used to create the many treasures of the Anglo-Saxon, Viking and Norman worlds were inherited from antiquity and continued in use, with some refinements, into medieval times. There is unfortunately no surviving Anglo-Saxon manuscript setting out the techniques and tools known to the smiths and other craftsmen, along with details of how to produce specific effects. Our only guide to understanding how the Anglo-Saxon smiths worked is to study the products of their labours.

Cabochon

Cabochon is a gem cutting and setting technique, whereby the stone is highly polished to form a flat underside and domed upper face, so that it is D-shaped in section. The stone is then placed on a metal (usually gold) base and a narrow collet is built around the rim; the collet has to be a very tight fit to secure the stone. The cabochon technique is normally used for larger stones which are to be displayed separately, as distinct from the cloisonné technique discussed below.

Carving

Carving is the removal of material with a sharp instrument. Anglo-Saxon craftsmen used various types of carving to produce masters and moulds, as well as to decorate bone, antler, wood, ivory, etc. Metal and wood items were often given a secondary carved surface to sharpen the finished surfaces; extreme examples of this are called 'chip-carved' where a series of flat surfaces have been created to give a glittery effect.

The degree of muscle control needed to produce fine carving is enormous, and there was no means to correct errors easily. The most detailed carvings were accomplished in wax, and the moulds were made by the cire perdue method. Occasionally there are finds of trial-pieces – scrap bones on which a design has been lightly carved to test it out before committing to work on the final item.

Casting

Casting is one of the oldest methods for the production of metal items. All fine metalwork began as a rough casting which was worked to produce the finished item. There are several casting techniques known to have been used in the Anglo-Scandinavian and Norman periods, of which open (single piece) moulds, bi-valve (matched two piece) moulds and lost-wax were the most common.

One-piece moulds were used for flat castings where detail was limited to one surface; they could be carved from bone, antler or clay.

Anglo-Saxon craftsmen produced two-piece moulds which were then luted with clay to produce a very strong matrix, with a high probability of a successful casting. Sophisticated two-piece moulds were used for more complex shapes, requiring detail on more than one surface, and to avoid undercutting. Craftsmen were able to introduce very fine detailing into their masters by careful use of stamps. There are few known examples of objects which can be shown to have come from the same mould.

In *cire perdue* (lost-wax) casting, a wax model was made, then covered with clay in which fine sand was mixed to prevent shrinkage, then heated to allow the wax to melt and run out through a prepared channel. Molten metal was poured into the void through one channel while the air escaped through a second one, and on cooling the metal will have taken on the shape of the cavity. One problem with this technique is air bubbles: if air is trapped in the mould it leaves a bulbous void on the surface, and if it has been trapped in the clay mould the sudden rise in temperature can cause it to explode.

Over time craftsmen developed a two-tier mould system whereby a wax model was formed in a mould, then detail added and the revised wax master was used in the *cire perdue* process.

Cloisonné

Cloisonné is a gem-setting technique which was favoured in the earlier Anglo-Saxon period.

It involves the cutting of precious stones (and other materials) into thin slabs and regular shapes which are then mounted into metal cells to form patterns; the cells differ from those used in champ-levé because they are formed from separate elements while champ-levé cells are gouged or stamped out of the metal surface – in other words, champ-levé is set into a recess in the metal surface while cloisons are built up above it. The only stone used in quantity by early Germanic smiths was garnet, although coloured glass, amber and bone were inserted for contrasting effect. The favoured metal was gold, and the cells were often only 1 mm high and 0.025 mm thick (i.e. on the Sutton Hoo material).

The method produced a flat face in which the upper surface of the stone was flush with the setting. The smith had to work carefully to ensure that while soldering one cell, he did not overheat the metal and destroy all the surrounding work. The advantage of cloisonné was that the surface of the stone was not obscured by any part of the setting, giving a clean effect. Anglo-Saxon cloisonné was perfected in the 7th century, at which time

some workshops were able to produce dazzling effects using tiny slips of stone and glass, just a few millimetres across, each set into a custom-made gold cell, with a stamped gold foil beneath the stone to give added sparkle.

The stones were cut with a fast-moving wheel and finished by hand into a 'step pattern' profile, so that they would interlock, and it is possible to relate the proportions of the steps to templates, and thus to individual smiths and workshops. Sometimes the stones were given a slight re-touching at the time of setting to ensure a better fit.

Chasing

Chasing is a metalworking technique, similar to punching and repoussé (both discussed below) but differing from the latter in that the metal is worked from the front. Chasing stretches the metal, and can produce fine adjustments to a repoussé design but has the effect of leaving tooling marks on the metal surface. By careful control of the tools, a fine textured surface could be produced.

Embossing

This technique involves the use of a positive die or former over which a thin sheet of metal is pressed or hammered to take on its shape and decoration. The metal used has to be soft and ductile – in the Anglo-Saxon case it would could be copper-alloy, silver or gold; with copper-alloy, often the surface was further treated by gilding or tinning. This technique was used for making Pressblech plates and other flat decorative items with low relief such as the backing plates for filigree.

Embossing differs from standard repoussé work in that it uses a die from which the design is transferred to the metal plate in a single operation while repoussé involves the careful building up of a design from the rear using stakes and punches.

Embossed figural pates were used to adorn high-status objects such as helmets and drinking horns in the 6th and 7th century; it was adapted to the production of high-status Christian items such as processional crosses. The plates were held in place with reeded bronze, and backed with pitch to ensure that they did not easily distort.

It is possible that some of the bone 'trial-pieces' found in settlements were actually used in the production of embossed decoration.

Embroidery

Few textiles remain from the Anglo-Saxon

and Norman periods, but there are some religious vestments which have been preserved. Woven in fine linen or wool, the textiles are often colourful with elaborate designs embroidered into the surface. The Bayeux Tapestry is in fact a huge embroidery in wool on a linen background.

Opus Anglicanum or 'English work' is a contemporary Latin term for very fine needlework produced in early medieval England, used on ecclesiastical and secular clothing, wallhangings and other textiles. It often comprises gold and silver threads on rich linen grounds. English embroidery was in great demand in medieval Europe.

Enamelling

This technique involves the preparation of a metal 'trough' into which glass is introduced; the piece is heated until the glass melts, forming a flat surface. Although known since ancient times, enamelling is not simple and requires careful control of the temperature in order not to melt the metal. On cooling, the surface is polished to leave a smooth, shiny and colourful effect. The champ-levé technique involves stamping the metal to create the trough, while the alternative cloisonné method involves constructing them it out of thin plate walls (as with cloisonné gem-setting).

The technique was not much used by early Anglo-Saxon craftsmen, as it had fallen out of favour by the 4th century AD in Roman Britain. It remained in use among the post-Roman Britons and is found decorating the escutcheons of hanging bowls which are a feature of 7th century high-status burials. There was also a localised centre of enamel production in the Cambridge area, which is found on some early Anglo-Saxon bow brooches.

Enamelling made a surprising return in the 11th century, when champ-levé appears on the surface of Anglo-Scandinavian cast disc brooches. After the severity of the previous Trewhiddle Style, which favoured silver and niello decoration, the introduction of champ-levé allowed the craftsman to experiment with colour. Enamelling remained a popular decorative technique into the Middle Ages.

Engraving

This technique involves the use of chisels of various sizes to remove metal from the surface. Anglo-Saxon craftsmen used line-engraving and relief-engraving techniques to decorate metal surfaces. The tools required included chisels, pitch blocks and some form of vice. The technique is essentially similar to woodcarving and some kinds of pottery decoration.

Fabrication

Fabrication is the construction of metal items out of separate plate components, often by soldering. In Anglo-Saxon contexts, it was only practised where craftsmen had access to sheet metal, which had to be produced by hammering out cast ingots or billets into flat sheets of even thickness. The thinned metal was frequently annealed to keep it workable. Extremely fine foils could be produced by skilled craftsmen: those behind high-quality garnet cloisonné work, for example, could be between 0.01 and 0.028 mm in thickness.

Filigree

Filigree is a technique for creating patterns using gold wire, often used with granulation. Both techniques were learnt from Roman, Pontic or Mediterranean craftsmen in the later Iron Age. The wire was hand-drawn down to the required thickness and soldered to the baseplate in lines, or twisted into 'ropework' threads. Often the ropework threads are laid so that the twists run in opposite directions, giving a chevron effect.

The solder had to be very carefully produced so that it would melt freely at a lower temperature than the gold wire; failure to get this right would melt the whole item. The solder was probably an alloy of lead and tin, applied in the form of a paste.

A variant of standard filigree was the beaded wire technique, whereby the wire was pressed to produce a series of spheres; the effect is similar to a line of granulation.

Gilding

Mercury gilding was in use in Anglo-Saxon workshops, where it was used to add lustre to the surfaces of silver and copper-alloy items. The extraordinary quality of Anglo-Saxon gilding accounts for the preservation of so many copper-alloy items which had received the treatment.

Mercury and powdered gold were mixed to a paste and applied to the surface to be gilded, which was heated to 356 degrees Celsius at which point the mercury would evaporate, leaving the gold fused to the metal surface below.

The presence of both enamel and niello on some gilded objects indicates that Anglo-Saxon craftsmen were able to plan the sequence of processes to achieve the desired results – these processes take place at higher temperatures than mercury gilding and would have destroyed the gilt surface. Alongside gilding, tinning was also practised, again using mercury, to produce a reflective, silvery surface.

Granulation

This technique involves melting a small amount of gold on a bed of charcoal until it forms a sphere; the surface of the sphere takes up some of the carbon, resulting in a lower melting point. The sphere is then soldered to the plain surface of the object, and the low melting point allows it to fuse with the surface at the point of contact.

Inlay

This technique consists of a channel cut or cast into the surface of a metal object, and a filled with a material of a contrasting colour. It was used on, for example, some iron spearheads in which silver wire was hammered to produce decorative or amuletic effects.

The results of the technique are easily masked by corrosion, and it was only in the 1950s that conservators began to notice its presence; with the development of radiographs, many iron items have been shown to have been inlaid.

The commonest inlay material in the Anglo-Saxon period is niello, a sulphide of silver applied as a paste which hardens to a glassy surface. Metal wire was also used, of often of silver softer than the iron into which it was to be hammered. To create the inlay channel, it was necessary to use a tool with a tip harder than the metal to be worked.

Aside from straightforward linear inlay, there is evidence for surface-inlay whereby a sheet of metal is applied to a keyed surface – a common practice for the discoid finials of great square-headed brooches. This process is known by its French name *damasquinure*. Another inlay technique found in early Anglo-Saxon England is *Tauschierarbeit* in which plain, polished iron is inlaid with a very complex pattern of fine silver wire motifs; this was used on the crest of the Sutton Hoo helmet and elsewhere.

Niello

Anglo-Saxon craftsmen routinely used niello for decoration, especially in the Middle Saxon period when the fashion was for shiny silver metalwork with designs reserved against a shiny black field. The preferred medium to produce the black background was niello, a sulphide of silver applied. It was applied as a paste and fired to harden it to a glassy surface. The use of niello declined when vitreous (glass) enamelling was re-introduced in the 11th century.

Pattern-Welding

This is a technique for the manufacture of sword blades which dates back to the 3rd century AD at least among the Germanic peoples. The principle is to twist together iron rods, and then to weld these rods together into a rough blank which is then further treated to produce the finished blade. Aside from swords, pattern-welding has been found on spearheads, but not on seaxes in England. The process may result in a more supple and springy blade, although modern experiments have shown that the mechanical advantage of pattern-welded over homogeneous blades has often been overstated.

The 'pattern' in pattern-welding is the surface effect caused by the welding together of rods of slightly varying quality (higher or lower carbon and phosphorus content), and the twisting of these rods so that the final blade bears a characteristic herringbone patterning. A comparable effect was achieved by damascening, whereby differing grades of iron were folded in on each other to produce a wavy effect, though the techniques are quite different in execution. In the pattern-welding process, a series of bi-metal twists are forged into short block of perhaps 1 cm square and a few centimetres long; alongside these are similarly shaped blocks in which the metal is not twisted but runs in straight parallel lines. These blocks are arranged according to the desired design, typically with straight blocks next to twisted blocks, in a sequence. These blocks may be split longitudinally and formed up in two layers, and offset so that the pattern on one side is offset against the pattern on the reverse. The blocks are then heated and forged together, while drawing the metal out to the desired length. The resultant pattern comprises the herringbone design with straight sections between the diagonals. To the blade is added a steel shoe, formed as a Y-shaped billet and forged onto the blade to create the cutting edge.

The twisting and folding action used on the rods would remove any remaining slag adhering to the metal (where the carbon would be in dangerously large clumps) and would further spread out the remaining small particles. Generally speaking, the higher the carbon content, the harder the metal will be, and so the better its cutting power and ability to retain its edge.

The technique was used on all the early swords recovered from Anglo-Saxon graves, but by the 9th century was no longer in favour. Later blades found in English cemeteries and rivers were not pattern-welded, but they sometimes feature inlaid inscriptions, the individual letters and shapes being made up by a pattern-welding process. Viking blades continued to be made in this manner into the 11th century.

Punching & Stamping

Punching and stamping are two methods of achieving decorative effects, which require special tools. Punches are simple metal rods with a shaped end which leave a negative impression when struck against the metal surface. The working ends of the punches have to be harder than the surface or they will deform. They probably had horn or wood handles over the upper end to make gripping them easier.

Careful and regular placement of the punch produced a satisfying, rhythmic result in the final design. Linear patterning using punches is called 'chasing' and is discussed above.

Punched or stamped patterns are among the commonest in Anglo-Saxon metalwork, but the range of designs is not large, with crosses, triangles and circles (pellets or discs) being the most popular. The commonest design of punch-mark on Anglo-Saxon and Viking metalwork was the pellet-in-triangle, with two variants: an isosceles triangle (with a longer base than sides), and an isosceles triangle with one slightly curved side (probably the earlier type). The pellets are placed in the angles of the triangle. Occasionally, a punch develops a distinctive deformity (distortion or chip) which allows the work of a single workshop to be traced on different items.

Stamping is a similar technique, used on pottery. The stamps may have been metalworking punches in some cases, but many were probably made from wood, bone or antler.

Reeding

Reeding is a method of corrugating or ribbing metal strips to strengthen them. These metal strips, mainly gold, are used in the construction of composite disc brooches, as well as for pendant loops. Likewise, reeded copper-alloy strips were used to secure the decorative plates to helmets. Some reeded strips are very fine, with the ribs less than 1 mm across. Exactly how they were produced is not known, but methods using swages and a clamp through which the metal plate is drawn are most likely.

Repoussé

This is a technique for raising a section of metal by hammering it from the rear. It can be used to produce a smooth, raised, moulded surface or to provide a textured background to a reserved foreground figure. It appears in the Middle Saxon period (i.e. on the crest of the Coppergate helmet). Some bracteates appear to have been raised using repoussé techniques.

Rivetting

Rivetting was used to combine separately made items. The rivets were formed from metal rod; in the case of jewellery items, this was usually copper-alloy but gold is also known. The rod itself was formed by drawing out a metal billet. It could be used for large items such as shield grips, or minute ones such as the decorated face of an applied disc brooch. Rivetting was used frequently to repair broken items, usually where soldering would involve a temperature high enough to damage the piece, and it was also sometimes built into the design of an item as a pleasing effect.

Silvering

The production of a sheer silver surface could be achieved in two ways. One was the application of a silver sheet with solder, the surface-inlay technique. Another involved fusing the foil to the cast metal surface; this has not yet been metallurgically examined to determine how it was achieved, but the result is similar to that of mercury gilding. The soldered-sheet technique was particularly used in conjunction with mercury-gilded surfaces, suggesting that the normal silvering process might damage the gilding.

Soldering & Brazing

Soldering was carried out by heating a soft solder – a metal with a lower melting point than the pieces to be joined – and allowing it to flow into the joint. Anglo-Saxon solder was based on lead or tin. Many brooches with appliqué panels and the walls of champ-levé enamel cells were assembled with solder. Brazing works on the same principle, but the pieces to be joined are heated and form a stronger bond with a fluxed solder; the flux may have been common salt.

Table of Image Sizes (in millimetres)

Type	Ref	Length	Width	Height	Diameter	Captions	Scale %
Image:	1.1.1-a	x	x	x	38.00	brooch; disc, lead, cruciform with central boss, in a German collection	150
Line Drawing	1.1.1-b	x	x	x	79.00	brooch; silver, nummular, Cuxton, Kent	50
Image:	1.1.1-c	x	x	x	20.24	brooch; silver, from a penny of Edward the Confessor, unknown findspot	200
Image:	1.1.1-d	x	x	x	39.00	mount; bronze, discoid, central motif of a regardant beast, Norwich, Norfolk	125
Image:	1.1.1-e	55.00	x	x	x	brooch; bronze, box, Urnes Style zoomorphic openwork, private collection	100
Image:	1.1.1-f	x	x	x	28.00	disc brooch; bronze, Borre style, Seighford, Staffordshire	125
Image:	1.1.1-g	x	x	x	27.00	disc brooch; bronze, Borre style, Dragonby, Lincolnshire	125
Image:	1.1.1-h	x	x	x	25.00	disc brooch; bronze, gilt, seven lobes, East Anglia	150
Image:	1.1.1-i	x	x	x	25.24	disc brooch; copper-alloy, cloisonné, 'hub-and-spokes' design, Lancashire	150
Image:	1.1.1-j	x	x	x	22.21	disc brooch; copper-alloy, cloisonné, Cambridgeshire	150
Image:	1.1.1-k	x	x	x	24.59	disc brooch; copper-alloy, Anglo-Scandanavian, Wiltshire	150
Image:	1.1.1-l	x	x	x	27.33	disc brooch; copper-alloy, Anglo-Scandinavian, Cambridgeshire/Suffolk border	150
Image:	1.1.1-m	x	x	x	25.59	disc brooch; copper-alloy, 'floral geometric' design, County Durham	150
Image:	1.1.1-n	x	x	x	24.18	disc brooch; copper-alloy, central panel in blue enamel, Lincolnshire	150
Image:	1.1.1-o	x	x	x	26.66	disc brooch; copper-alloy, outer bosses on outer ring, Cambridgeshire	150
Image:	1.1.1-p	x	x	x	24.67	disc brooch; copper-alloy, cloisonné, floral pattern, Suffolk	150
Image:	1.1.1-q	x	x	x	25.32	disc brooch; copper-alloy, enamelled, Anglo-Scandinavian, East Anglia	150
Line Drawing	1.1.1-r	x	x	x	44.00	disc brooch; central champ-levé panel; Bedlington, Northumberland	100
Image:	1.1.1-s	x	x	x	20.71	nummular brooch; copper-alloy, William I, Cambridgeshire	150
Image:	1.1.1-t	x	x	x	17.92	nummular brooch; copper-alloy, Hampshire	200
Image:	1.1.2-a	42.34	x	x	x	plate brooch; copper-alloy, quadrangular, Lincolnshire	100
Image:	1.1.2-b	38.99	x	x	x	plate brooch; copper-alloy, lozengiform, radiating floral decoration, Suffolk	100
Image:	1.1.2-c	66.00 - 71.00	x	x	x	plate brooch; bronze, elliptical, pair, tortoise shape, findspot unknown	100
Image:	1.1.2-d	79.00	x	x	x	plate brooch; bronze, elliptical, tortoise shape, Alnwick, Northumberland	100
Image:	1.1.3-a	39.30	x	x	x	zoomorphic brooch; copper-alloy, openwork, bird, Cambridgeshire	150
Image:	1.1.3-b	35.05	x	x	x	zoomorphic brooch; copper-alloy, openwork, bird, North Wickford, Essex	150
Image:	1.1.3-c	29.00	x	x	x	zoomorphic brooch; cast silver, punched-point lines, unknown findspot	150
Image:	1.1.3-d	37.00	x	x	x	zoomorphic brooch; bronze, bird standing on branch, unknown findspot	150
Image:	1.1.3-e	31.00	x	x	x	zoomorphic brooch; bronze, Valkyrie and Horseman, Nottingham	150
Image:	1.1.3-f	95.00	x	x	x	trefoil brooch, bronze, private collection	100
Image:	1.1.3-g	81.00	x	x	x	trefoil brooch, gilt-bronze, private collection	100
Image:	1.1.4-a	37.55	x	x	x	penannular brooch; copper-alloy, zoomorphic terminals, Hampshire	125
Image:	1.1.4-b	30.46	x	x	x	penannular brooch; silver, rectangular terminals, Baltic area	150
Image:	1.1.5-a	27.58	x	x	x	annular brooch; copper-alloy, gilt, angel wrestling with a lion, unknown findspot	150
Image:	1.2-a	35.20	x	x	x	buckle; copper-alloy, Scandinavian Baltic type, Lincolnshire	125
Image:	1.2-b	23.67	x	x	x	buckle; copper-alloy, bird-head feature flanked by curved wings, Suffolk	150
Image:	1.2-c	20.44	x	x	x	buckle; copper-alloy, Anglo-Scandinavian, dished D-shaped loop, Yorkshire	200
Image:	1.2-d	37.62	x	x	x	buckle; copper-alloy, openwork, Urnes Style, human head, Sleaford, Lincolnshire	150
Image:	1.2-e	41.14	x	x	x	buckle; copper-alloy, rectangular, Scandinavian type, Kemble, Gloucestershire	150
Image:	1.2-f	32.10	x	x	x	buckle; copper-alloy, hinged, two-piece, triangular beast-head, unknown findspot	150
Image:	1.2-g	44.68	x	x	x	buckle; copper-alloy, Romanesque Style animal, north Essex	125
Image:	1.2-h	41.00	x	x	x	buckle; copper-alloy, rectangular plate and animal-head, Cambridgeshire	150
Image:	1.2-i	30.42	x	x	x	buckle; copper-alloy, sharply-beaked bird-head, Cambridgeshire	150
Image:	1.2-j	27.54	x	x	x	buckle; copper-alloy, sharply-beaked bird-head, Cambridgeshire	150
Image:	1.2-k	26.60	x	x	x	buckle; copper-alloy, beast with a muzzle, Snettisham, Norfolk	150
Image:	1.2-l	35.00	x	x	x	buckle plate; Romanesque style, lion facing outwards, Dirk Kennis collection	125
Image:	1.2-m	42.64	x	x	x	buckle; copper-alloy, elliptical loop, human mask, Marlborough, Wiltshire	125
Image:	1.2-n	46.03	x	x	x	buckle; copper-alloy, with plate, strap end, Hertfordshire	125
Image:	1.2-o	24.21	x	x	x	buckle; copper-alloy, zoomorphic, two drooping animal heads, Cambridgeshire	150
Image:	1.2-p	44.87	x	x	x	belt mount; copper-alloy, two lions rampant, acquired London, 1990	200
Image:	1.2-q	54.22	x	x	x	belt mount; copper-alloy, sea lion regardant, acquired London 1988	200
Image:	1.3-a	33.52	x	x	x	strap end; silver-gilt, cross with central boss, Netherlands	150
Image:	1.3-b	38.36	x	x	x	strap end; copper-alloy, Winchester style, East Anglia	150
Image:	1.3-c	62.97	x	x	x	strap end; copper-alloy, zoomorphic, animal-head finial with open mouth, Norfolk	125
Image:	1.3-d	32.02	x	x	x	strap end; copper-alloy, Thomas's Class E type 1 variant, Cossington, Somerset	150
Image:	1.3-e	47.00	x	x	x	strap end; knotwork animal executed in openwork, Dirk Kennis collection	150
Image:	1.3-f	27.64	x	x	x	strap end; copper-alloy, stylised male face, East Anglia	150
Image:	1.3-g	34.00	x	x	x	strap end; silver-gilt, Winchester style, Salisbury, Wiltshire	150

Type	Ref	Length	Width	Height	Diameter	Captions	Scale %
Image:	1.3-h	53.00	x	x	x	strap end; bronze, bifacial animal mask, Birchington, Kent	125
Image:	1.3-i	49.99	x	x	x	strap end; copper-alloy, two rampant beasts, central tree, Wiltshire	125
Image:	1.3-j	40.52	x	x	x	strap end; copper-alloy, addorsed ravens emerging from base, Norwich, Norfolk	125
Image:	1.3-k	28.83	x	x	x	strap end; copper-alloy, Ringerike Style, East Anglia	150
Image:	1.3-l	40.75	x	x	x	strap end; copper-alloy, long-necked bird amid foliage, Hastings, Sussex	150
Image:	1.3-m	39.89	x	x	x	strap end; copper-alloy, zoomorphic, hunting dog finial, Suffolk	150
Image:	1.3-n(a)	42.82	x	x	x	strap end; copper-alloy, ball-ended, expanding profile, Skirpenbeck, Yorkshire	125
Image:	1.3-n(b)	37.15	x	x	x	strap end; copper-alloy, ball-ended, expanding profile, Skirpenbeck, Yorkshire	125
Image:	1.3-n(c)	40.60	x	x	x	strap end; copper-alloy, ball-ended, raised rib inner edge, Skirpenbeck, Yorkshire	125
Image:	1.4-a	91.42	x	x	x	pin; copper-alloy, tapering, hinged annular head, Nottingham	100
Image:	1.4-b	x	x	x	22.00	pinhead; copper-alloy, domed, animal decoration, Dirk Kennis collection	150
Image:	1.4-c	12.19	x	x	x	pinhead; silver-gilt, four gold foil panels, North Ormsby, Lincolnshire	300
Image:	1.4-d	102.00	x	x	x	dress pin; copper-alloy, Romanesque beast-head terminals, Sussex	100
Image:	1.5-a	36.00	x	x	x	pendant; silver, elite horseman with hawk, continental Europe	125
Image:	1.5-b	24.72	x	x	x	pendant; silver, lunulate, continental European origin	150
Image:	1.5-c	30.07	x	x	x	pendant; copper-alloy, gilt, crouching hound, Hastings, Sussex	150
Image:	1.5-d	39.61	x	x	x	pendant; copper-alloy, lunulate bifacial, two beasts, Tilbury, Essex	150
Image:	1.6-a	50.35	x	x	x	mount; bronze, open rectangle, triangular openwork extension, Norfolk	125
Image:	1.6-b	x	x	x	19.67	mount; copper-alloy, discoid stud, griffin, Fakenham, Norfolk	150
Line Drawing	1.6-c	60.00	x	x	x	mount; copper-alloy, horse and rider, Charwood, Leicestershire	100
Image:	1.6-d	38.40	x	x	x	mount; copper-alloy, Anglo-Scandinavian, cloisonné centre, Essex	200
Image:	1.6-e	50.00	x	x	x	mount; bronze, horse's head with hatched mane, near York, Yorkshire	100
Image:	1.6-f	x	x	x	31.00	mount; silver, discoid, Hiberno-Norse type, findspot unknown	125
Image:	1.6-g	35.43	x	x	x	belt loop; copper-alloy, elliptical, cross pattée and four creatures, Norfolk	125
Image:	1.6-h	63.00	x	x	x	mount; bronze, leaping beast, Dirk Kennis collection	100
Image:	1.6-i	36.83	x	x	x	mount; copper-alloy, D-section, Burnham Market, Norfolk	150
Image:	1.6-j	60.08	x	x	x	mount; bronze, complex interlaced zoomorphic panel, East Yorkshire	200
Image:	1.6-k	26.24	x	x	x	mount; coppper-alloy, gilt, bird with three-toed feet, East Anglia	150
Image:	1.6-l	35.67	x	x	x	mount; copper-alloy, openwork, beast with open jaws, Hampshire	125
Image:	1.6-m	48.12	x	x	x	mount; copper-alloy, Scandinavian Urnes Style openwork, Kent	125
Image:	1.6-n	26.87	x	x	x	mount; copper-alloy, serpentine creature curled into a circle, Suffolk	200
Image:	1.6-o	60.89	x	x	x	mount; copper-alloy, serpentine creature curled into a circle, Scandanavia	150
Image:	1.6-p	41.66	x	x	x	mount; copper-alloy, serpentine creature in Urnes Style, Suffolk	150
Image:	1.6-q	37.14	x	x	x	mount; copper-alloy, openwork, bifacial, two opposing beasts, Suffolk	150
Image:	1.6-r	70.73	x	x	x	mount; copper-alloy, Anglo-Scandinavian version of Urnes Style, Essex	100
Image:	1.6-s	43.90	x	x	x	mount; copper-alloy, horse and rider, Kent	150
Image:	1.6-t	20.05	x	x	x	mount; copper-alloy, animal head, Wiltshire	300
Image:	1.6-u	28.00	x	x	x	mount; copper-alloy, zoomorphic, Surrey collection	150
Image:	1.6-v	43.42	x	x	x	mount; copper-alloy, quatrefoil with fleur-de-lys shaped lugs, Norfolk	125
Image:	1.6-w	32.46	x	x	x	mount; bronze, human bust, Yorkshire	150
Image:	1.6-x	34.95	x	x	x	mount; copper-alloy, gilt, Romanesque Style beast-head, acquired London 1994	250
Image:	1.6-y	70.00	x	x	x	mount; bronze, serpentine creature within vegetation, Kennis collection	100
Image:	1.6-z	18.75	x	x	x	mount; copper-alloy, stylised head, Staffordshire	200
Image:	1.6-aa	38.00	x	x	x	mount; bronze gilt, human-headed beast mount, South Yorkshire	150
Image:	1.7-a	x	x	x	x	finger ring; gold, Hiberno-Norse, unknown	not to scale
Image:	1.7-b	x	x	x	20.64	finger ring; electrum, formed as a single lozengiform sheet, Humberside	150
Image:	1.7-c	x	x	x	23.85	finger ring; gold, multiple strands and punchmarks, Tostock, Suffolk	150
Image:	1.7-d	x	x	x	20.42	finger ring; copper-alloy, lozenge-shaped band, punched ring-and-dot, Norfolk	150
Image:	1.7-e	x	x	x	29.15	finger ring; copper-alloy, ring-and-dot motifs, Suffolk	150
Image:	1.7-f	24.93	29.13	x	x	finger ring; gold, cross moline bezel, Buriton	125
Image:	1.7-g	29.12	x	x	x	finger ring; copper-alloy, moulded decorative twists, Derbyshire	125
Image:	1.7-h	29.00	x	x	x	finger ring; gold, plaited wire, Scandinavian origin, findpot unknown	125
Image:	1.7-i	23.94	x	x	19.38 ID	finger ring; copper-alloy, gilt, two pairs of opposed spirals, Baltic area	125
Image:	1.7-j	23.00	x	x	x	finger ring; silver, decorated with filigree and granulation, Baltic origin	125
Image:	1.7-k	x	x	x	20.59	finger ring; silver, ribbed, Lehtosalo-Hilander's Type III, continental Europe	150
Image:	1.7-l	x	x	x	17.65	finger ring; copper-alloy, expanding-band, strap-and-boss style, continental Europe	150
Image:	1.7-m	25.00	x	x	21.43 ID	finger ring; gold, raised median band, continental Europe, Yorkshire collection	125
Image:	1.7-n	27.27	x	x	x	finger ring; gold, lozengiform bezel with stamped decoration, continental Europe	125
Image:	1.7-o	28.00	x	x	20.46 ID	finger ring; gold, lozengiform, punched decoration, old European collection	125
Image:	1.7-p	24.50	x	x	x	finger ring; formed from three wires, continental Europe, American collection	125
Image:	1.7-q	25.00	x	x	19.84 ID	finger ring; gold, plain bar lower hoop, three expanding rods, continental Europe	125
Image:	1.7-r	29.45	x	x	x	finger ring; gold, plait in three bands each of two gold rods, continental Europe	125
Image:	1.7-s	x	x	x	21.05	finger ring; silver, double zigzag pattern, continental Europe	150
Image:	1.7-t	21.35	x	x	18.00 ID	finger ring; silver, stirrup-shaped, decorated shoulders, unknown findspot	150
Image:	1.7-u	23.32	x	x	18.70 ID	finger ring; silver-gilt, two stylised animal heads, unknown findspot	125

Type	Ref	Length	Width	Height	Diameter	Captions	Scale %
Image:	1.7-v	x	x	x	88.00	bracelet; gold, twisted expanding rods, old European collection	75
Image:	1.8.1-a	970	x	x	x	sword hilt; silver with bronze, Petersen's Type H, private collection	not to scale
Image:	1.8.1-b	21.45	x	x	x	sword pommel terminal; silver-gilt, Petersen Type O/R, unknown findspot	150
Image:	1.8.1-c	57.60	x	x	x	sword pommel; copper-alloy, Baltic findspot	125
Image:	1.8.1-d	48.00	x	x	x	sword pommel; silver, Petersen's Type S, Scandinavia	125
Image:	1.8.1-e	58.00	x	x	x	sword pommel; bronze, Brazil-nut, Nottinghamshire	125
Image:	1.8.1-f	26.96	x	x	x	sword pommel; bronze, five parallel lobes and two horn finials, Fakenham, Norfolk	200
Image:	1.8.1-g	61.90	x	x	x	sword pommel; bronze, five separate lobes, plain channels between, Lincolnshire	100
Image:	1.8.1-h	88.62	x	x	x	sword hilt guard; copper-alloy, elliptical, Hampshire	75
Image:	1.8.1-i	910	x	x	x	sword; iron, narrow blade and fuller, from an American collection	not to scale
Image:	1.8.1-j	142 Hilt	x	x	x	sword; iron, pattern-welded blade, three-lobe pommel, Scandinavian origin	100
Image:	1.8.1-k	1010	x	x	x	sword; iron, narrow blade, Brazil-nut pommel, continental Europe	not to scale
Image:	1.8.1-l	970	x	x	x	sword; iron, thin blade, Petersen's I Type hilt, from Scandinavia	not to scale
Image:	1.8.1-m	880	x	x	x	sword; iron, 'Type L' hilted, three-lobed pommel, Cornwall, river find	not to scale
Image:	1.8.1-n	970	x	x	x	sword; iron, type X pommel, continental Europe	not to scale
Image:	1.8.1-o	50.12	x	x	x	sword pommel; copper-alloy, Oakeshott's Type F, Stretham, Ely, Cambridgeshire	150
Image:	1.8.1-p	34.73	x	x	x	sword pommel; copper-alloy, wheel type, enamelled heraldic designs, Essex	150
Line Drawing	1.8.2-a	300 approx	x	x	x	axe; iron, curved profile, Museum of London	not to scale
Image:	1.8.3-a	250 approx	x	x	x	spearhead, iron inlaid silver wire; American collection	not to scale
Image:	1.8.3-b	300 approx	x	x	x	spearhead, iron parcel-gilt; American collection	not to scale
Image:	1.8.3-c	300 approx	x	x	x	spearhead, iron parcel-gilt; American collection	not to scale
Image:	1.8.4-a	300	x	x	x	knife; iron, seax, Wheeler's Type II/III, Barrington, Cambridgeshire	50
Image:	1.8.4-b	129	x	x	x	knife; iron, triangular-section blade with a shallow curvature, Hertfordshire	100
Image:	1.8.4-c	25.39	x	x	x	knife pommel; copper-alloy, slotted type, Kent	125
Image:	1.8.4-d	30.00	x	x	x	knife pommel; bronze, flat in section, Essex	125
Image:	1.8.5-a	64.00	x	x	x	sword belt fitting; bronze, three voids and knotwork, continental Europe	100
Line Drawing	1.8.5-b	65.79	x	x	x	scabbard chape; copper-alloy, Baltic Scandinavian type, continental Europe	100
Image:	1.8.5-c	32.26	x	x	x	scabbard chape; copper-alloy, Romanesque Style figural, Essex	125
Image:	1.8.5-d	43.02	x	x	x	rectangular plate; copper-alloy, figure left facing, acquired London 1981	200
Line Drawing	1.8.5-e	39.50	x	x	x	chape; zoomorphic, Suffolk	150
Image:	1.8.5-f	33.27	x	x	x	scabbard mount; copper-alloy, helmeted figure, Norfolk	150
Image:	1.8.5-g	46.45	x	x	x	chape or scabbard mount; copper-alloy, Woods's Type 1B, Cambridgeshire	150
Image:	1.8.5-h	26.19	x	x	x	scabbard mount; copper-alloy, Woods's Type 3B, York	150
Line Drawing	1.8.5-i	28.20	x	x	x	scabbard mount; copper-alloy, triangular, Amesbury Wiltshire	150
Line Drawing	1.8.5-j	49.00	x	x	x	scabbard mount; copper -alloy, J-shaped, Exeter	100
Line Drawing	1.8.5-k	30.50	x	x	x	scabbard mount; copper-alloy, triangular, Hampshire	150
Image:	1.8.5-l	66.11	x	x	x	dagger chape; copper-alloy, stylised horseman and bird, Cambridgeshire	100
Image:	1.8.5-m	38.57	x	x	x	sheath mount; copper-alloy, knife, Winchester Style, Buckinghamshire	150
Image:	1.8.5-n	36.00	x	x	x	scabbard or sheath mount; copper-alloy, Woods's Type 3B, Hampshire	150
Image:	1.8.5-o	35.00	x	x	x	sheath mount; copper-alloy, dagger, Woods's Type 3B, Co.Durham collection	150
Image:	1.8.5-p	34.83	x	x	x	sheath chape fitting; copper-alloy, Woods's Type IB, Tilbury, Essex	150
Line Drawing	1.8.5-q	38.00	x	x	x	sheath chape fitting; winged beast, North Yorkshire	150
Image:	1.8.5-r	42.41	x	x	x	sheath chape; copper-alloy, dagger, quadrupeds and bulbs, Norfolk	150
Image:	1.8.6-a	49.13	x	x	x	mace head; bronze, narrow collar, rows of spikes, Castle Hedingham, Essex	100
Image:	1.8.6-b	73.09	x	x	x	mace head; copper-alloy, twelve spikes, Sheffield, Yorkshire	75
Image:	1.8.6-c	91.00	x	x	x	mace head; iron, inlaid silver, Scandinavian origin	100
Image:	1.8.6-d	53.00	x	x	x	mace head; iron, lozengiform panels, Cambridgeshire	75
Image:	1.8.7-a	180.00	x	x	195.00	helmet; iron, four-plate riveted conical, continental Europe	75
Image:	1.9.1-a	55.36	x	x	x	stirrup mount; copper-alloy, Williams's Class A, serpentine decoration, Suffolk	100
Image:	1.9.1-b	42.60	x	x	x	stirrup mount; copper-alloy, Class B, Type 4, Kennis collection	100
Image:	1.9.1-c	46.00	x	x	x	stirrup mount; copper-alloy, 'male-face' type, Kennis collection, Norfolk	100
Image:	1.9.1-d	48.00	x	x	x	stirrup mount; copper-alloy, Williams's Class B Type 4, found Norfolk	100
Image:	1.9.1-e	60.00	x	x	x	stirrup mount; copper-alloy, Williams's Class A Type 2, Norfolk	75
Image:	1.9.1-f	32.02	x	x	x	stirrup mount; copper-alloy, Williams's Class B Type 3, Group 1, Eye, Norfolk	100
Image:	1.9.1-g	61.00	x	x	x	stirrup mount; copper-alloy, Williams's Class A, from an American collection	100
Image:	1.9.1-h	35.54	x	x	x	stirrup mount; copper-alloy, Williams's Class A Type 1, Cambridgeshire	100
Image:	1.9.1-i	42.90	x	x	x	stirrup mount; copper-alloy, Williams's Class A Type 1, Hertfordshire	100
Image:	1.9.1-j	24.04	x	x	x	stirrup mount; copper-alloy, Williams's Class A Type 6, unknown findspot	100
Image:	1.9.1-k	44.04	x	x	x	stirrup mount; copper-alloy, Williams's Class B Group B, Norfolk	100
Image:	1.9.1-l	42.81	x	x	x	stirrup mount; copper-alloy, Williams's Class A Type 13, Essex	100
Image:	1.9.1-m	48.52	x	x	x	stirrup mount; copper-alloy, Williams's Class A Type 12, Cambridgeshire	100
Image:	1.9.1-n	45.27	x	x	x	stirrup mount; copper-alloy, Williams's Class A Type 1, continental Europe	100
Image:	1.9.1-o	46.00	x	x	x	stirrup mount; copper-alloy, Williams's Class B Group 3, Norfolk	100
Image:	1.9.1-p	48.00	x	x	x	stirrup mount; Williams's Class B Type 4, from an American collection	100
Image:	1.9.1-q	47.58	x	x	x	stirrup mount; copper-alloy, human male advancing, right hand above dog, Suffolk	100

Type	Ref	Length	Width	Height	Diameter	Captions	Scale %
Image:	1.9.1-r	35.37	x	x	x	stirrup mount; copper-alloy, Ringerike style, Norfolk	150
Image:	1.9.1-s	44.64	x	x	x	stirrup mount; copper-alloy, hollow in the form of an animal head, Suffolk	100
Image:	1.9.1-t	38.83	x	x	x	terminal; copper-alloy, beast-head detailing, Hampshire	100
Image:	1.9.1-u	35.37	x	x	x	terminal; copper-alloy, beast-head detailing, Snettisham, Norfolk	125
Image:	1.9.1-v	44.64	x	x	x	terminal; copper-alloy, beast-head detailing, Haverhill, Suffolk	100
Image:	1.9.2-a	31.13	32.11	x	x	bridle pendant; copper-alloy, rearing horse,Lincolnshire	125
Image:	1.9.2-b	90.29	x	x	x	cheek piece; copper-alloy, Ringerike Style, Hertfordshire	75
Image:	1.9.2-c	63.00	x	x	x	strap fitting; copper-alloy, tri-lobed ends, punched-line, Dragonby, Lincolnshire	100
Image:	1.9.2-d	47.96	x	x	x	harness pendant; bronze, two wolves, Thetford, Norfolk	100
Image:	1.9.2-e	47.28	x	x	x	horse pendant; copper-alloy, two dragon heads, Lincolnshire	100
Image:	1.9.3-a	x	x	140 / 145		stirrups; iron, continental Europe	not to scale
Line Drawing	1.9.3-b	x	132	230.00	x	stirrup; iron, inlaid copper-alloy decoration, River Cherwell, Oxford	not to scale
Image:	1.9.4-a	61.00	x	x	x	prick spur; bronze, Gooderstone, Norfolk	100
Image:	1.9.4-b	160.00 ea.	x	x	x	prick spurs; iron Carolingian Frankish, continental Europe	not to scale
Image:	1.9.4-c	150.00	x	x	x	prick spur; iron, looped sockets with lozengiform outer plates, Suffolk	not to scale
Image:	1.9.4-d	100.00	x	x	x	prick spur; copper-alloy, copper and silver inlay, continental workmanship	100
Image:	1.9.4-e	130.00	x	x	x	prick spur; iron, rectangular-section pricket, Lancashire	50
Image:	1.9.5-a	116.00	x	x	x	horseshoe; iron, elongated arched plan, raised stops, Chepstow castle, Wales	75
Image:	1.10-a	x	x	x	72.38	reliquary mount; silver plate, copper-alloy backing, North East England	100
Image:	1.10-b	14.01	x	x	x	book mount; gold, 'fleur de lis' pattern, old European collection	250
Image:	1.10-c	30.63	x	x	x	cross; silver, central disc, branching arms with spherical finials, unknown findspot	150
Image:	1.10-d	59.00	x	x	x	mount; gilt-bronze, Limoges, Suffolk	100
Image:	1.10-e	60.78/59.70/58.88/58.61/40.48	x	x	x	plaques; bronze, Limoges, findspot unknown	100
Image:	1.10-f	42.00	x	x	x	book mount; copper-alloy, 'howling wolf', Kennis collection	125
Image:	1.10-g	x	x	x	36.84	papal bull; lead, Pope Alexander III, Norwich, Norfolk	100
Image:	1.10-h	x	x	x	37.18	papal bull; lead, Pope Lucius III, Essex	100
Image:	1.10-i	38.90	x	x	x	plate or mount; copper-alloy, polychrome champ-levé design, Nottinghamshire	150
Image:	1.10-j	57.32	x	x	x	plaque for cross; copper-alloy, Limoges, winged lion of St Mark, Cambridgeshire	100
Image:	1.10-k	110.00	x	x	x	bronze cast Corpus Christi; Norwich, Norfolk	100
Image:	1.10-l	75.00	x	x	x	mount; copper-alloy Limoges, churchman in his mantle, Kennis collection	100
Image:	1.10-m	58.00	x	x	x	mount; copper-alloy Limoges, churchman in his mantle, Alderton, Suffolk	100
Image:	1.10-n	64.00	x	x	x	mount; copper-alloy Limoges, churchman in his mantle, continental Europe	100
Image:	1.10-o	54.87	x	x	x	mount; copper-alloy Limoges, churchman in his mantle, Co. Durham	100
Image:	1.10-p	39.83	x	x	x	mount; copper-alloy, male in classical robes, East Anglia	125
Image:	1.10-q	80.00	x	x	x	mount; copper-alloy, Limoges, churchman in his mantle, continental Europe	100
Image:	1.10-r	30.00	x	x	x	mount; copper-alloy, Limoges, Kennis collection, West Midlands	200
Image:	1.10-s	57.14	x	x	x	mount; copper-alloy, T-shaped, Sutton-on-the-Hill, Derbyshire	100
Image:	1.11-a	37.00	16.00	49.50	x	gaming piece; bronze, horse and rider with teardrop shield, Nottinghamshire	200
Image:	1.12 -a	19.00	x	x	x	weight; copper-alloy, polyhedral, inset garnet cloisons and a gold annulet	200
Image:	1.12-b	x	x	x	16.86	weight; copper-alloy, Scandinavian 'barrel' profile, Norfolk	200
Image:	1.12-c	18.92	x	x	x	weight; copper-alloy, conical, Cambridgeshire	200
Image:	1.12-d	x	x	x	16.10	weight; lead with embedded copper-alloy stud, York, Yorkshire	200
Image:	1.12-e	49.07	x	x	x	gold bar; hack bullion, findspot unknown	100
Image:	1.12-f	78.61	x	x	x	ingot; alloy of lead and copper, Stamford Bridge, Yorkshire	75
Image:	1.12-g	34.48	x	x	x	seal matrix; lead, pendant, Tilbury, Essex	125
Image:	1.13-a	83.00	x	x	x	candle holder; bronze, dog, Norman Sicilian workmanship, Netherlands	75
Image:	1.13-b	58.00	x	x	x	figure; bronze, standing dog, Somerset	100
Image:	1.13-c	18.11	x	x	x	bead spacer; silver, Scandanavia	150
Image:	1.13-d	43.63	x	x	x	handle; copper-alloy, for firesteel, East Anglia	125
Image:	1.13-e	47.65	x	x	x	latch key; copper-alloy, rotating, Nottinghamshire	125
Line Drawing	1.13-f	126.00	x	x	x	padlock key; copper-alloy, barrelled shaft and three bars	75
Image:	1.13-g	90.00	x	x	x	key; bronze with inlay, Thames foreshore at Billingsgate	100
Image:	1.13-h	55.00	x	x	x	key; bronze, casket, decorated, Nottinghamshire	100
Image:	1.13-i	54.00	x	x	x	key; bronze, casket, openwork, Catterick, Yorkshire	125
Image:	1.13-j	70.00	x	x	x	key; bronze, barrel, with suspension loop, Catterick, Yorkshire	100
Image:	1.13-k	100.00	x	x	x	handle; bronze, openwork, floral frame, Sicily (?)	100
Image:	1.13-l	57.00	x	x	x	lock-plate; gilt bronze, beast-head top, Cambridgeshire	125
Image:	1.13-m	86.69	x	x	x	handle; knife or tool, dragon's head, Norfolk	100
Image:	1.13-n	33.46	x	x	x	swivel terminal; ribbed, Hampshire	150
Image:	1.13-o	35.52	x	x	x	swivel mount rings; bronze, zoomorphic, Lincolnshire	150
Image:	1.13-p	45.17	x	x	x	swivel-mount rings; copper-alloy, Lincolnshire	125
Image:	1.13-q	63.71	x	x	x	swivel mount rings; bronze, zoomorphic, Lincolnshire	125
Image:	1.13-r	71.64	x	x	x	swivel; copper-alloy, pyramidal openwork, Fen Drayton, Huntingdonshire	100
Image:	1.13-s	44.87	x	x	x	swivel mount rings; bronze, zoomorphic, Norfolk	125
Line Drawing	2.2.1-a	x	x	x	x	Runestone; St. Pauls, London	not to scale

4. Glossary

Anglo-Norman
The culture of England after the Norman invasion, roughly AD 1066-1134

Anglo-Saxon
Shorthand term for the West Germanic cultures of Britain, contrasted with the North Germanic or Viking

Anglo-Scandinavian
The culture of Anglo-Saxon England during the period of Danish domination (roughly AD 1015-1035)

Anglo-Saxon Chronicle
(ASC) a series of documents, all based on a single original, relating the history of the English from the 5th century up to the 11th century, and in some examples into the 12th century

annular
Ring-shaped

annulet
Decorative motif in the form of a circle

anthropomorphic
Shaped like a human being

beading
Decoration in which a series of pellets is placed in a series like beads on a thread

Beowulf
Anglo-Saxon poem about a hero who overcomes three monsters; set in southern Scandinavia, written in its present form about AD 1000

biconical
Shaped like two cones set mouth-to-mouth

billeted
decorated with (sub-)rectangular blocks

boss
Metal cup on a shield which protects the hand, and any hemispherical projection

bow
Part of a long brooch which is bent round in a semi-circle to accommodate the bunching of the cloth beneath

brooch
Clothes fastener in which the pin and clasp are hidden behind a decorated face-plate

cabochon
(French) method of setting a hemispherical stone whereby it is gripped by a metal collar at the base leaving the top proud of its cell

champ-levé
(French) decorative technique whereby cells are created in the surface of an object and filled with coloured enamel, creating a panelled effect

chape
Metal fitting from the lower end of a sword's scabbard

chip-carving
Style of metalwork in which high-relief details are produced by lost-wax casting, and then sharpened with chisels and files

cloison
Decorative stone set into a metal cell

copper-alloy
Archaeological term describing any of the many alloys of copper used in Roman and Anglo-Saxon times, including bronze and brass

cruciform
Cross-shaped

Danegeld
Payments made to the Vikings in return for peace

Domesdæg
'Doomsday' – the book compiled under the direction of William I to record the ownership of property in 11th century England

enamel
Decorative glass-based paste

escutcheon
Decorative roundel or plate, usually with a hook for attaching a chain

Exeter Book
Book of English poems presented to Exeter Cathedral in the 11th century, where it remains today

filigree
Decoration consisting of twisted (usually gold) wire soldered to a metal surface

FLO
Finds Liaison Officer under the PAS.

Francia
The Frankish state, corresponding to most of modern France, Netherlands, Belgium and Germany

futhorc
(or fuþorc) Anglo-Saxon runic alphabet

granulation
Decoration consisting of tiny (less than 1 mm diameter) balls of gold soldered to a metal surface; often accompanies filigree

grog
Filler material used in the production of pottery, often sand, grass or shell

guilloche
Decorative motif consisting of circles linked by S-shaped designs

headrail
Garment worn by married Anglo-Saxon women, consisting of a long rectangle of cloth placed over the crown of the head, the ends draped over one or both shoulders, and secured by hairpins at the temples

Hiberno-Norse
Culture of the Vikings in Ireland, and of Irish culture during the period of Norse domination Hiberno-Saxon Culture of the Anglo-Saxons influenced by the Irish, mainly in art styles, lettering, book production, etc.

inhumation
Burial rite in which the body is laid in the ground, sometimes in a coffin, usually wearing clothes and accompanied by grave-goods such as weapons (male) and jewellery (female)

interlace
Decoration in which bands pass over and under each other

knotwork
Decorative motif in which bands loop over and under each other, similar to interlace but the bands are continuous

Lacnunga
Anglo-Saxon medical manuscript

loop
Part of a buckle against which the tongue is held

lost-wax casting
Production method in which a wax master is covered in clay to make a mould, the wax is melted out and the void is filled with molten metal. Normally the mould has to be broken to remove the product.

lunulate
Shaped like a half-moon or crescent

mailcoat
Hauberk, an armoured garment made from ringmail

mask

Decorative motif consisting of a face (human or animal) shown facing the viewer straight-on

millefiori

(Italian) Slices of coloured glass rod, drawn and fused usually in a chequer pattern

niello

Silver-based paste which is applied to metalwork; it hardens to a glassy black surface

openwork

Decoration in which metal is removed to form a hole, either cast or by later piercing

PAS

Portable Antiquities Scheme

palmette

Fan-shaped motif made from curling lines

pattern-welding

Technique for producing sword-blades in which bars of different grades of iron are twisted and forged together

pellet

Decorative motif based on a flat disc

pelta

Shape like a fan or axe-blade with inward-curving sides and an outward-curving outer-edge

penannular

Shaped like an incomplete circle or horse-shoe plate   Part of a buckle which attaches the loop to the belt or strap

pommel

Top part of a sword-hilt which acts as a counter-balance to the blade

punching

Decoration of metalwork with repeated impressed patterns

quincunx

An arrangement of five items set at the four corners and the centre of a square, like the spots on a '5' playing card

regardant beast

Animal seen in profile, its head turned to look backwards to its own tail, which is often raised to meet its muzzle

repoussé

(French) Decoration of metalwork with the design pushed out from behind

ring-and-dot

Motif consisting of a circle with a central dot

ringmail

Armour made from interlinked rings

ropework

Design made of S-shaped elements in series like the bands of a rope

roundel

Decorative motif based on an open circle, or annulate

runes

Germanic alphabet of 24 characters; the Anglo-Saxon version extended this to 28, and subsequently to 33 in Northumbria

saltire

Decorative motif of a cross (+) turned through 45 degrees (x)

scutiform

Shaped like a shield, a flat disc with a domed centre

seax

Anglo-Saxon knife or single-edged sword

segmented

Describes a surface divided into discrete sections

seriation

Development of an artefact-type over time, forming the basis of typology and relative dating

spatulate

Widening towards the outer edge, shaped like a shovel (opposite of tapering)

strap-divider

A metal fitting attached at the point where straps meet or cross to strengthen the joint.

tang

Part of a sword- or knife-blade which is fitted inside the hilt

tongue

Part of a buckle which pierces the fabric of the belt or strap

triskele
Decorative motif consisting of three legs set in a spiral procession

typology
Study of an artefact class to establish the main types, and the variants within these

vandyke
Decorative plate in the form of an elongated triangle

volute
Shape consisting of two spirals joined by a c-shaped bridge

Younger Fuþark
Scandinavian runic alphabet of 16 letters

zoomorphic
Shaped like an animal

5. Bibliography

Abbreviations
AJ   Antiquaries Journal
ASSAH   Anglo-Saxon Studies in Archaeology & History
JBAA   Journal of the British Archaeological Association
JMH   Journal of Medieval History
Med. Arch. Medieval Archaeology

Abels, R. **Bookland and Fyrd Service in Late Saxon England** in **S. Morrillo** (ed.), 1999

Bachrach, B. **The Feigned Retreat at Hastings** in **S. Morrillo** (ed.), 1999

Backhouse, J., Turner, D.H. & Webster, L. **The Golden Age of Anglo-Saxon Art 966-1066**, London, 1984

Bersu, G. and Wilson, D.M. **Three Viking Graves in the Isle of Man (Society of Medieval Archaeology Monograph 1)**, London, 1966

Bork, R. (ed.) et al., **De Re Metallica: The Uses of Metal in the Middle Ages, AVISTA Studies in the History of Medieval Technology, Science and Art, vol. 4**, Aldershot, 2005

Cameron, E. **Sheaths and Scabbards in England AD 400-1100, BAR British Series 301**, Oxford, 2000

Carpenter, D. **The Struggle for Mastery: Britain 1066-1284**, London, 2003

Chibnall, M. **Military Service in Normandy Before 1066** in **S. Morrillo** (ed.), 1999

Coatsworth, E. & Pinder, M. **The Art of the Anglo-Saxon Goldsmith, Fine Metalwork in Anglo-Saxon England: its Practice and Practitioners**, Woodbridge, 2002

Cook, B. & Williams, G. (eds.) **Coinage and History in the North Sea World, c. AD 500-1200. Essays in Honour of Marion Archibald, Brill**, 2006

Cramp, R. & Miket, R. **Catalogue of the Anglo-Saxon and Viking Antiquities**, Newcastle-upon-Tyne, 1982

Crowson, R., Lane, T., Penn, K. & Trimble, D. **Anglo-Saxon Settlement on the Siltland of Eastern England, Lincolnshire Archaeology and Heritage Reports Series no.7**, Sleaford, 2005

Dodwell, C.R. **Anglo-Saxon Art: A New Perspective**, Manchester, 1982

Douglas, D.C., **William the Conqueror: the Norman Impact upon England**, Berkeley, 1964

Ellis Davidson, H.R. **The Sword in Anglo-Saxon England**, Woodbridge, 1962 (reprint 1994)

Ewing, T. **Gods and Worshippers in the Viking and Germanic World**, Stroud, 2008

Forte, A., Oram, R. & Pedersen, F. **Viking Empires**, Cambridge, 2005

Fuller, J.F.C. **The Battle of Hastings, 1066** in **S. Morrillo** (ed.), 1999

Gillingham, J. **William the Bastard at War** in **S. Morrillo** (ed.), 1999

Gillmor, C. **Naval Logistics of the Cross-Channel Operation, 1066** in **S. Morrillo** (ed.), 1999

Gilmour, B. **Swords, Seaxes and Saxons: Pattern-Welding and Edged Weapon Technology from Late Roman Britain to Anglo-Saxon England** in **Henig & Smith**, (eds.) 2007

Glover, R. **English Warfare in 1066** in **S. Morrillo** (ed.), 1999

Gooch, M. **The Cross on Viking Coins** in **CCNB Newsletter no. 48**, 2009

Graham-Campbell, J. **Bossed penannular brooches: a review of recent research** in **Med. Arch**. 1975
-   **The Viking World**, London, 1980

Graham-Campbell, J., Hall, R., Jesch, J. & Parsons, D.N. **Vikings and the Danelaw. Select Papers from the Proceedings of the Thirteenth Viking Congress**, Oxford, 2001

Grainge, C.& G. **The Pevensey Expedition: Brilliantly Executed Plan or Near Disaster?** in **S. Morrillo** (ed.), 1999

Grills, H. **The Life and Times of Godwine, Earl of Wessex**, Swaffham, 2009

Hallam, E.M. **Domesday Book Through Nine Centuries**, London, 1986

Hamerow, H. & MacGregor, A. **Image and Power in the Archaeology of Early Medieval Britain. Essays in Honour of Rosemary Cramp**, Oxford, 2001

Hammond, B.M. **British Artefacts, vol.1**, Witham, 2009
-   **British Artefacts, vol.2**, Witham, 2010

Hårdh, B. **Silver in the Viking Age: A Regional Economic Study, Acta Archaeologica Lundensia series in 8o no.25**, Stockholm, 1996

Haywood, J. **Encyclopaedia of the Viking Age**, London, 2000

Henig, M & Smith T.J. (eds.) **Collectanea Antiqua: Essays in Memory of Sonia Chadwick Hawkes,**

BAR International Series 1673, Oxford, 2007

Henson, D. **The English Élite in 1066 – Gone But Not Forgotten**, Hockwold-cum-Wilton, 2001

Hinton, D. **Catalogue of the Anglo-Saxon Ornamental Metalwork 700-1100 in the Department of Antiquities**, Ashmolean Museum, Oxford, 1974
- **Gold and Gilt, Pots and Pins: Possessions and People in Medieval Britain**, Oxford, 2005

Hodges, R. **Dark Age Economics. The Origins of Towns and Trade AD 600-1000**, London, 1989

Hume, D. **The History of England** in S. Morrillo (ed.), 1999

Indruszewski, G. & Godal, J. **Maritime Skills and Astronomic Knowledge in the Viking Age Baltic Sea** in **Studia Mythologica Slavica vol.IX**, Ljubljana, 2006

Jessup, R. **Anglo-Saxon Jewellery**, Aylesbury, 1974

Karkov, C.E. **The Archaeology of Anglo-Saxon England: Basic Readings**, London, 1999

Kennett, D.H. **Anglo-Saxon Pottery,** Princes Riseborough, 1989

Kerr, M.&N. **Anglo-Saxon Architecture,** Princes Riseborough, 1983

Kershaw, J.F., **Culture And Gender in the Danelaw: Scandinavian and Anglo-Scandinavian Brooches in Viking and Medieval Scandinavia vol.5**, 2009

Krapp, G.P. & van Kirk Dobbie, E. (eds.) **The Exeter Book, Anglo-Saxon Poetic Records, vol. 3**, New York, 1936

Kruse, S. **Ingots and Weight Units in Viking Age Silver Hoards** in **World Archaeology, Vol. 20, No. 2, Hoards and Hoarding**, 1988

Lang, J. **Anglo-Saxon Sculpture,** Princes Risborough, 1988

Leahy, K. **Anglo-Saxon Crafts**, Stroud, 2003

Lehtosalo-Hilander, P.-K. **Luistari, 4 vols**, Helsinki, 1982

MacGregor, A. **Bone, Antler, Ivory and Horn. The Technology of Skeletal Materials Since the Roman Period**, London, 1985

MacGregor, A. & Bolick, E. **A Summary Catalogue of the Anglo-Saxon Collections (Non-Ferrous Metals),** B.A.R. British Series 230, Oxford, 1993

MacGregor, A. et al, **A Summary Catalogue of the Continental Archaeological Collections**, Oxford, 1987

Mason, E. William Rufus: **Myth and Reality in JMH 31**, 1977
- **William II: Rufus, the Red King**, London, 2005.

Messent, J. **The Bayeux Tapestry Embroiderers' Story**, Thirsk, 1999

Morrillo, S. Hastings: **An Unusual Battle** in S. Morrillo (ed.), 1999
- (ed.) **The Battle of Hastings. Sources and Interpretation**, Woodbridge, 1999

Moskowich-Spiegel, I. **Scandinavians and Anglo-Saxons: Lexical Substitution and Lexical Change in English, Fòrum de Recerca, vol.10**, Castelló, 2005

Owen Crocker, G.R. **Dress in Anglo-Saxon England**, Woodbridge, 2004

Peirce, I. **Swords of the Viking Age**, Woodbridge, 2004

Pollington, S. **Rudiments of Runelore**, Hockwold-cum-Wilton, 1995
- **Leechcraft - Early English Charms, Plantlore and Healing**, Hockwold-cum-Wilton, 2000
- **The English Warrior from Earliest Times till 1066**, 2nd edition, Hockwold-cum-Wilton, 2002
- **The Mead-Hall – Feasting in Anglo-Saxon England**, Hockwold-cum-Wilton, 2003

Pollington, S., Kerr, L. & Hammond, B. **Wayland's Work – Anglo-Saxon Art and Material Culture from the Fourth to the Seventh Century**, Swaffham, 2010

Richards, J.D., Jecock, M., Richmond, L. & Tuck, C. **The Viking Barrow Cemetery at Heath Wood, Ingleby, Derbyshire in Med.Arch.**, 1995

Robinson, J. **The Lewis Chessmen**, London, 2004

Rundkvist, M. **Domed oblong brooches of Vendel Period Scandinavia** (open source book ark:/13960/t61557f41), 2010

Ryan, M. (ed.) **Ireland and Insular Art AD 500-1200**, Dublin, 1987

Sykes, N. **The Zooarchaeology of the Norman Conquest in Anglo-Norman Studies 27: Proceedings of the Battle Conference**, 2004

Vince, A G & Bayley, J. **A Late Saxon Glass Finger Ring from the City of London,** Trans. London & Middlesex Archaeological Society, vol. 34, 1983

Wallace, P.F. and Ó Floin, R. **Treasures of the National Museum of Ireland**, Dublin, 2002

Weber, K. **Byzantinische Münzgewichte Materialkorpus für 1-Nomisma-Gewichte, Studien zur Vielfalt der Ausführungsform Metrologie und Herstellung**, Schwelm, 2009

White, A.J. **Copper-Alloy Combs from Britain and Frisia in Med. Arch., vol. XXXII**, London, 1988

Wilson, D.M. **Some neglected late Anglo-Saxon swords in Med.Arch. vol. IX**, 1965
- (ed.) **The Northern World. The History and Heritage of Northern Europe. AD 400-1100**, London, 1980
- **The Vikings and Their Origins**, London, 1989
- **The Vikings in the Isle of Man**, Aarhus, 2008

Wood, M. **In Search of England**, London, 2000

Woods, P. **Chape Research Project Reports, 1-8** in *The Searcher*, 2006-9
- **A Group of Late Saxon and Early Norman Dagger Chapes in Med.Arch.**, (forthcoming)

Youngs, S. (ed.) **'The Work of Angels': Masterpieces of Celtic Metalwork, 6th-9th Centuries AD**, London, 1989

6. Index

128

7. About the Author

More than thirty years ago, as a regular visitor to London's collectors' markets and provincial coin fairs, Brett Hammond formed an interesting collection of ancient British coins and antiquities. He progressed to part-time dealing, with stalls and tables at several venues where he gained a reputation for the variety of his stock, and for his willingness to pass on his knowledge of Celtic, Romano-British and Anglo-Saxon material cultures to all who came to browse, to buy from him, and to share the pleasures of collecting antiquities.

Following a period in the USA, where he witnessed the enthusiasm of many American collectors for ancient European history and artefacts, he returned to the UK determined to expand his business; to include the artefacts of other cultures in his stocks; and to reach out across the world for more collectors to add to his client base. Brett launched TimeLine Originals in the 1990s, just as the internet, email, digital photography and online buying and selling were transforming the collecting world and the dealing in coins and artefacts. At the company's Upminster headquarters he gathered experts in photography, digital imaging, web design and artefact conservation. He also engaged the services of several specialists whose knowledge complemented his own.

The company developed a world-wide clientele of both buyers and sellers. Many clients, together with the families and executors of deceased clients, looked to the company when seeking to dispose of collections and single items. An increasing number of general and trade sellers also began to approach the company, seeking access to the company's extensive mailing lists. By late 2009, the decision was taken to launch TimeLine Auctions, with Brett as CEO, to provide new opportunities for clients at all levels to buy and sell coins and artefacts of all periods and cultures.

Brett Hammond also contributes editorial features and articles to a number of publications with national and international readerships, he is continuing work on his *British Artefacts* series of books and he has co-authored *Wayland's Work*. His ownership of the award-winning Wildwinds database, which now holds almost 67,000 images of ancient coins as a resource for collectors, shows his love for and commitment to the aim of thirty years ago: to share the pleasures and rewards of finding and collecting ancient coins and antiquities.

BRITISH ARTEFACTS
VOLUMES 1 & 2

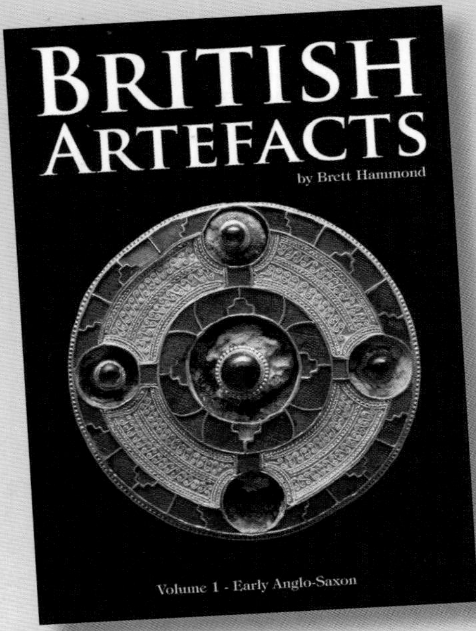

British Artefacts Volume 1 – Early Anglo-Saxon *by Brett Hammond*
The early Anglo-Saxon period is the Cinderella of English history sandwiched as it is between the more "glamorous" late Roman and mid-Saxon periods.
However, the years covered by this work saw huge changes in the social structures, settlement patterns, political ideology, language and religion in lowland Britain. The main evidence for the material culture for the period comes from finds of metalwork and the objects covered in **British Artefacts** make it an ideal reference work for detectorists, archaeologists, museum staff, collectors and anyone with a serious interest in the early Anglo-Saxon years.
The book contains 20 maps showing the distribution throughout Britain of various classes of objects and has 240 beautiful illustrations. The contents show the breadth of coverage of the title: Intro to the Series, Glossary, Intro to the Early Anglo-Saxon Period, Advice for Collectors, Valuations, Runes, Advice for Finders, Outline of the Early Anglo-Saxon Period, Art styles, Artefacts production & distribution, Ceramic production and Metal Artefacts.
The "Metal Artefacts" covered include: Brooches, Buckles & Belt Fittings, Clasps, Weapons & Fittings, Bowls & Vessels, Pendants, Belt Rings, Bracelets & Arm-rings, Chatelaines, Latch-lifters & Girdle-Hangers, Keys, Combs, Earrings, Finger-rings, Harness & Bridle Mounts, Neck-rings, Padlocks, Pins, Purse Mounts & Fire-steels, Pyxides, Spoons, Spurs, Tags, Metallic Threads, Toilet Sets, Tools and Weaving Equipment.
The Non-Metallic Artefacts include Amber, Antler, Bone, Ceramics, Gemstones, Glassware, Horn, Ivory and Stone.
A4, 132 pages, £15.00, ISBN 978 1 897738 351
Quote from Celtic coin dealer Chris Rudd. "Thank you very much indeed for sending me a copy of British Artefacts Vol. 1. Like all Brett Hammond enterprises, this book exudes quality – quality research, quality writing, quality illustration, quality production. It is a magnificent book – a work of Early Anglo-Saxon art and a work of art in its own right. This is more than an authoritative reference book; it is a compulsive and pleasurable read for anyone remotely interested in the period. Well done, Brett!"

British Artefacts Volume 2 – Middle Saxon & Viking *by Brett Hammond*
The first volume in the series dealt with the early material from the Adventus Saxonum through to the middle of the 7th century when the process of conversion to Christianity was underway.
This second volume covers the Middle Saxon material, including the impact that the Vikings had on Anglo-Saxon life during the period of the Great Army, the resistance of King Alfred, the Danelaw and its reconquest by Edward the Elder, the Kingdom of York and the formation of England under King Athelstan.
The chapter headings sum up the contents: The Middle Saxon & Viking Period; Runes & Roman Script; Artefact Production & Distribution; Art Styles; Advice for Collectors; Advice for Finders; Metal Artefacts – including brooches, buckles, strap ends, fasteners & tags, pendants, mounts, rings & bracelets, weapons & fittings, ecclesiastical & liturgical items, gaming pieces, weights, keys, tools & utensils; Non-Metallic Artefacts; Anglo Saxon & Viking Burials; Middle Saxon & Viking Kingdoms – all lavishly illustrated with nearly 400 beautiful colour pictures and maps.
The book is laid out logically with preliminary discussions of the history, and of manufacturing and distribution as well as advice for collectors and finders; there follows a brief outline of the scripts, Roman and runic, Anglo-Saxon and Scandinavian. The art styles are discussed in some detail, then follow the metal artefacts by type, followed by the non-metallic material such as glass, amber, bone and horn. The burial traditions – inhumation and cremation, Viking and Anglo-Saxon – are handled succinctly in a few pages with typical grave plans. Scandinavian settlement is dealt with as well as the Middle Saxon and Viking kingdoms. Finally the summary data for the images are tabulated, followed by a glossary, bibliography and index.
The book covers the subject brilliantly, offers a great breadth of material and manages to spring a few surprises – it includes a unique gold finger ring bearing the name Cynefrid, a gilded Irish mount and some spectacular swords.
A4, 148 pages, £15.00 ISBN 1 897738 382

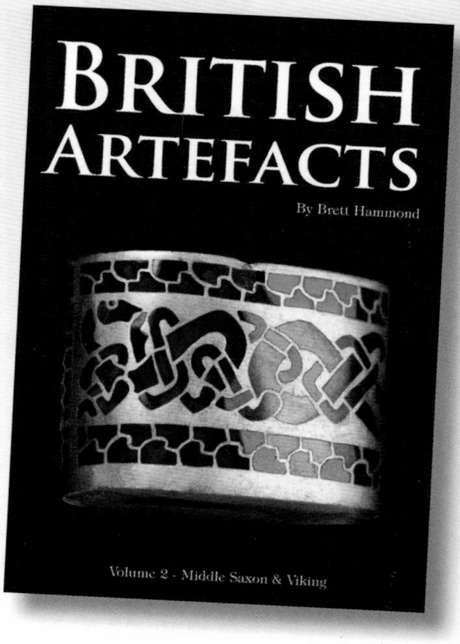

order online www.greenlightpublishing.co.uk
orders 01376 521900
by post to Greenlight Publishing, 119 Newland Street, Witham, Essex CM8 1WF